D0948390

BLACK, BLIND, & IN CHARGE

A Story of Visionary Leadership and Overcoming Adversity

GOVERNOR DAVID A. PATERSON

Skyhorse Publishing

To view the photo gallery, use a QR code scanner app on
your phone or go to www.BlackBlindAndInCharge.com

Skyhorse Publishing books may be purchased in bulk at special discounts for sales
promotion, corporate gifts, fund-raising, or educational purposes. Special editions
can also be created to specifications. For details, contact the Special Sales
Department, Skyhorse Publishing, 307 West 36th Street, 11th Floor, New York,
NY 10018 or info@skyhorsepublishing.com.

Skyhorse® and Skyhorse Publishing® are registered trademarks of Skyhorse
Publishing, Inc.®, a Delaware corporation.

Visit our website at www.skyhorsepublishing.com.

10 9 8 7 6 5 4 3 2 1

Library of Congress Cataloging-in-Publication Data is available on file.

Cover design by Brian Peterson
Cover photo credit: Getty Images

Print ISBN: 978-1-5107-5633-5
Ebook ISBN: 978-1-5107-6309-8

Printed in the United States of America

Dedication

This book is dedicated to the people of
New York whom I have been honored to
serve for several decades of my life, and to the people
of my home town; Harlem.

David A. Paterson

Contents

Contents

Acknowledgments

Dr. Simon E. Mills, for facilitation, collation,
writing, re-writing, branding, and guiding of this book.

Ed Breslin, for his coaching, development,
and additional writing.

Prologue
Marching with the Greatest

Saturday, June 14, 1986:

I was standing on a makeshift stage at the corner of 125th and Adam Clayton Powell Jr. Boulevard, formerly Seventh Avenue, in Harlem. The Adam Clayton Powell State Office Building, behind the makeshift stage, was going to be the launching point for one of many marches that will be conducted throughout New York City. All of these marches would culminate in a big rally in Central Park. The purpose of the marches and the big rally was to condemn the apartheid conditions that still existed then in South Africa: more specifically, to challenge the American banks and corporations that had money invested in South Africa to withdraw such economic support to this racist country.

Harlem activists such as Elombe Brath, Queen Mother Moore, Ann Rocker, Barbara Barber, Pork Chop Davis, Marshall England, and Mary Madison were sprinkled throughout the crowd, spreading enthusiasm. Harlem royalty was present as well: three of the four members of the Gang of Four were marching in the parade: David Dinkins, Charles Rangel, and my father, Basil Paterson, were all present and accounted for. The only missing member, Percy Sutton, made fewer public appearances since becoming the owner of Inner City Broadcasting. Although he couldn't attend in person, both of his radio stations were covering the event. David Dinkins, then the Borough President of Manhattan, was going to co-chair the march along with tennis star Arthur Ashe. Congressman Charles Rangel would lead the delegation of elected officials that included Assemblyman Danny Farrell, Assemblywoman Geraldine Daniels, City Councilman Hilton Clark—and myself, a newly-minted state senator.

Basil Paterson, former state senator and my father, because of his usual modesty and his typical shunning of the spotlight, had eschewed the opportunity to march, but he was hard at work behind the scenes with others to orchestrate the opening of the parade. Jim Bell, head of The Coalition of Black Trade unionists, was set to lead the marchers. Officials of the Transport Workers Union and the United Healthcare Workers Union were busy helping Bill Lynch, the famous organizer from Local 1707 of the AFSCME, the union of state, county, and municipal workers, to finalize plans for the beginning of the march. Bill had recently left the union to serve as the deputy borough president to Dinkins.

It was a blustery, cold morning, but the sun shone bright and full, and as the march began around midday, it was clear that the temperature would warm the crowd. That would help, but what really heated up the crowd was a rumor that the two guest grand marshals, Borough President David Dinkins and tennis star Arthur Ashe, would be joined by a special guest, Muhammad Ali.

Ali was my childhood idol. I had practiced dancing around the ring the way he did, sometimes even backpedaling like the Greatest of All Time. I had also recited his poetry, reveled in his humor, and stood loyal when he opposed the Vietnam War by refusing Selective Service in 1967, a short two and a half years after he became the youngest heavyweight champion of all time by knocking out Sonny Liston. The commissioners of boxing then stripped him of his title for refusing, as a conscientious objector, to step forward for induction into the army at Selective Service headquarters. As it turned out, the commissioners had stripped him of his title illegally. His valiant effort to regain the championship after the Supreme Court upheld his conscientious objector status in 1970 resulted in his narrow loss at Madison Square Garden to Joe Frasier, in one of the more epic fights in boxing history on March 8, 1971.

But a few years later Ali succeeded in regaining the title, only the second man ever to do so, in a shocking upset victory over George Foreman in Kinshasa, the capital of Zaire. Ali then defended his title several times, eventually losing it, only to regain it for a third time, at an advanced age, the only man ever to pull off this unbelievable feat. After his retirement, he became a global leader for causes like civil rights and world peace, the elimination of poverty, and the eradication of hunger, despite contracting the deadly Parkinson's disease and other health-impairing injuries from boxing that impeded his lifestyle and diminished his energy. But he never quit his quest for universal justice, dignity, and peace for all people of every color, race, country of origin, ethnicity, creed, or religion.

This was my favorite human being. I would have been happy enough just to have the opportunity to shake his hand. But as the beginning of the march approached and the crowd swelled with enthusiasm, there was a great deal of noise and activity around me, a good bit of it hectic and confusing. And, for some reason, my chief of staff Geoffrey Garfield had stepped away and left me standing there alone. Some people came up to me, shook my hand, and congratulated me for becoming a state senator at such a young age.

This had been an incredible year. Back on April 19th 1985, I had served my last day as an assistant in the Queens District Attorney's office. Though I had not yet passed the bar, I was an active candidate for admission to the bar and in that capacity had tried cases in criminal court and held hearings in Supreme Court. This experience had been invaluable. But I had then left the DA's office to work on the borough president's campaign with Dinkins. I was his fundraiser during the summer. I learned a lot about politics that year and a lot about campaigns. There was one incident in which I was asked— along with Geoff Garfield, who also worked at the campaign, and along with another volunteer who happened to be named Spike Lee—to set up tables because the New York State Black and Puerto Rican legislative caucus was going to have a meeting in the campaign headquarters. Incidentally, Spike Lee at this time was simply Spike Lee, not yet *the* Spike Lee; his first breakout movie, *She's Gotta Have it,* would not be released until a short while later. In any event, little did I know while setting up the tables and introducing myself to some of the senators and assembly members who were in the meeting, that the next time they would meet, which would be in December of 1986, I would be sitting at the table among them as one of the members.

What had happened was this: In the meantime, a confluence of coincidences combined with an unusual number of events to create an opportunity for me to run, win, and become a state senator. At thirty-one, I was the youngest state senator at that time and one of the five youngest to ever achieve this position. So, a number of amazing things were happening to me that year, embodied at that moment by this march, which, penultimate to my being elected and sworn into the state Senate, was the most amazing event I had experienced to this point. Apparently, I was unaware that one of the people whose hand I shook as I was preparing to march in the rally, was Muhammad Ali, who seemed puzzled by the fact that I didn't really acknowledge him other than to shake his hand, say hello, and keep moving.

He then said to a bunch of people gathered around him, "Now I can see why these elected officials are out of touch, this guy over here doesn't even know who I am."

As the story goes, Borough President Dinkins, who later became the first African-American Mayor of the city of New York, stepped up and informed Ali that I am blind and probably did not notice that he was who he was. Ali became upset that he had cracked this joke about a person who had a severe sight disability so he came over to me. As he approached, there were about fifteen people with him, and I realized instantly who he was. He took my right hand and held it in both of his hands and asked me a question that I did not really understand. He then leaned down and whispered into my ear, "Would you march with me." I was flabbergasted, completely taken by surprise, and for an instant speechless, but then I did manage to reply, "I would love to march with you." He escorted me to the front of the parade. He then stood on the end of the front line, I was in the middle, Arthur Ashe was to my left, and David Dinkins anchored the other end as we begin to parade down Adam Clayton Powell Boulevard, marching down Adam Clayton Powell Boulevard.

I was just trying to maintain equilibrium after this unforeseen experience, but I could hear the other marchers, mostly longstanding elected officials, complaining about why an individual who'd only been in office three and a half months is marching in the front line and they are marching behind me. They were muttering this sort of thing: "I've served in the assembly for seven years and this is an outrage, who does he think he is, who the xxxx allowed him to march in the front of the parade?" Ali seemed aware of the chattering from the rear as well and asked me, "What's all this about?"

"They're complaining because I'm in the front of the line and I'm the youngest elected official here."

"Well," Ali said, "I was the youngest heavyweight champion of the world. You should be here."

Now I was on Cloud Nine, but as marchers started to approach 116th Street, Ali began to tire: He had his arm around my shoulder but he was beginning to lean on me. I think at the time Ali may have weighed somewhere between 270–280 pounds. I believe I weighed, soaking wet, 145 pounds. So, obviously, this arrangement couldn't go on too long with me able to hold him up and march at the same time. At one point Jim Bell and my father, monitoring things by walking backward at the head of the parade, stopped the march and approached Ali and asked if he felt well. He didn't actually say that he did; he said only, "I have to march." They asked me if I felt well and I wasn't going to give up this place in the parade for anything, I would be carried out of there before I would stop, so I just repeated what he said: "I have to march too." Ali and I marched on, but as we passed 112th Street, he was clearly fading, tired, and almost hanging on me; I was straining too, trying to maintain my balance as Geoff Garfield, my chief aide, came over and observed how red my face was getting.

In a whisper, I acknowledged Geoff's concern, but my mind harkened back to a fight I had once seen Ali in. He was the champion defending against the Olympic medalist, Leon Spinks, and Leon Spinks was ahead in the fight. Then, in the fifteenth round, Ali hit Spinks with a couple of good punches and it looked like he would knock Spinks out. But there was one problem: Ali himself was exhausted and out of gas. Spinks was so out of gas he couldn't retaliate and just stood there. You got the feeling that a stiff wind from any direction and both fighters would have fallen down from exhaustion. And I thought to myself, *Here I am battling it out with Muhammad Ali, and the only question is who's going to go first.* But Ali pressed on, as did I.

Finally, at 110th Street, as we entered Central Park, Ali's security team decided to take him out of the march. They were not as comfortable with him walking through the park on uneven terrain as they had been when he was just marching on the street, and so they took Ali away. Immediately I had that feeling of dizziness when a great weight has been taken from you, and I staggered until one of Ali's handlers stabilized me. "Was he too much for you?" the handler asked. Ali was about to get in the car and I said loud enough for him to hear, "Was he too much for me? He was too much for Sonny Liston, he was too much for Joe Fraser, he was too much for George Foreman—of course, he was too much for me." Turning to get in the car, Ali started laughing, sat down, and closed the door. I said to myself, *Time to die, all my missions have been achieved: I made Muhammad Ali laugh.*

ON THE MORNING of June 4, 2016, the news was read to me by my then-girlfriend, Mary Sliwa—now my wife. About an hour later my daughter Ashley called to tell me how sorry she was to hear about the passing of Muhammad Ali.

I asked her, "What made you call me?"

She said, "Because I knew how special he was to you."

At that point, I could feel uncontrollable tears.

A FEW WEEKS after the rally I was at a function sponsored by the Reverend Al Sharpton when someone put their hand on my right shoulder. It was Muhammad Ali. I got up and hugged him, very flattered that he recognized me, and even more enthused that I recognized him this time. That was the last time I ever saw him. But the circumstances from our magical march back in April provided the paramount example of the recurrent themes that have been engrained in the scroll of my life, what Deepak Chopra calls "conspiracies of improbability," or what many others call being in the right place at the right time.

THIS STORY ABOUT Muhammad Ali begins with me being unable to recognize him, at that time, the most recognizable person on the planet. Conspiracies of improbability can also mean being in the wrong place at the wrong time. And yet, Ali, who was known for his sensitivity to those with hardship, embraced me with warmth and charity. This kindness was reviled by those whose attendance at the rally for freedom could be explained by a desire self-promotion. My desire to march that day derived from my compulsion to stand up for justice, but I would be remiss if I denied myself the pleasure of striding between two global idols. Even though the champ's weight exhausted me, I wasn't going to relinquish this spotlight for anything. In the end, the world's best-known individual was enchanted by my imitation of him, which drew laughter. Meanwhile, inside I was chuckling at how I had cleverly achieved the goal my jealous colleagues were seeking, by promoting myself.

So these are the sweet and sour results of God's blessings that allowed me to live on this earth:

Frequent inability to recognize the obvious,

The recipient of charity from people with very big hearts,

The victim of enmity from people with very small minds,

An eminent desire to stand up for what is right,

Turning a blind eye to the reality that situations and tasks are overwhelming,

An innate need for attention and love to confirm my participation in life,

A willingness to encounter any discomfort in pursuit of a goal,

Never showing an unwillingness to move tables and chairs, regardless of my stature, or to perform other menial tasks, if doing so enables the achievement of a larger goal: the collective prize, that is, and not the individual trinket, and always being a person who has proven publically and privately that when I've made mistakes, I can freely admit when I'm wrong.

Above all, I smile whenever I think of my encounter with my "greatest" hero. For my entire life, I have reveled in humor, and in fact, it's the basis of my love of life, which is inexhaustible. As you read this book, as you read about my conspiracies of improbability, both good and bad, bear in mind the one essential tool you need to keep handy in life, especially when your own conspiracies of improbability get a bit too heavy: your sense of humor. That, and if you happen to be black and blind, you'd better be in charge.

1

What Do You Mean I'm the Governor?

Monday, March 10, 2008:

I was the lieutenant governor of New York, serving under Elliot Spitzer. Elected November 7, 2006, I was two months into my second year in this role. The day before, a quiet Sunday, strangely enough, I cleaned up my entire house: All my files under my bed, all the inner cleaning you don't usually do. Since it was a really quiet Sunday I invited my family to dinner; we went to a restaurant known as the Ocean Grille, on 79th Street and Columbus Avenue. Three of the four of us had a relaxing glass of wine, all except my son Alex, who to this day is not a drinker. We didn't have these types of dinners often, but everybody had a good time and the next morning, my daughter Ashley, on spring break, flew off to Aruba on vacation with friends. My son went to school, my wife Michelle went to work, and I went off into history, but I just didn't know it yet. With a state trooper driving my official car we headed to my office in Albany. My assistant David Johnson was in the passenger's seat and I sat in the back listening to the morning column by Fred Dicker in the *New York Post*.

Around 10:30 in the morning I got a phone call in my office informing me that there was a family planning event being held at the convention center in Albany, and the governor's secretary asked me to attend in place of the governor because his trip to Albany had been delayed. I told them that I was actually very busy and would have appreciated more notice. The reality is the lieutenant governor is never busy. But I told them this anyway because everyone appreciates proper notice and a timely heads-up.

Lieutenant governors are first in line to succeed the governor should the governor be unable to serve, but lieutenant governors are last in line in terms of consultation, responsibility, or respect. Although it's also true that in this case Governor Spitzer probably gave me the greatest role that any lieutenant governor has had in recent memory. I was working on energy policy, stem cell research, domestic violence prevention, arts and culture, and also on minority and women's business enterprises, trying to get more procurement of state contracts to these businesses, which were woefully underrepresented. Nonetheless, lieutenant governors don't do very much. I often quipped at appearances that the lieutenant governor's job was to wake up every morning at 6:30 and call the governor's mansion. If the governor answered, your work was done for the day.

Oddly enough, I only learned after I was elected lieutenant governor that there is an organization known as The National Lieutenant Governor's Association. The association actually holds a couple of conferences every year. I attended one. At the conference, Governor Jim Risch of Idaho, who at the time of this writing is now serving as the junior senator for Idaho, told us that every year or two a governor leaves office and is replaced by a lieutenant governor, that it happens more often than you think, and that we should all be prepared to assume the governorship should this actually occur.

In May of 2006, Jim Risch was serving as lieutenant governor of Idaho under Governor Dirk Kempthorne when President Bush tapped Governor Kempthorne for the cabinet post of Secretary of the Interior. When Governor Kempthorne resigned to become Secretary of the Interior, Jim Risch became the governor of Idaho for the remainder of Kempthorne's term. So Jim Risch served as the governor of Idaho for seven months from May 2006 to January 2007. That's how he knew all about a sudden elevation from lieutenant governor to governor. In the 2007 election in Idaho, Jim Risch re-won the office of lieutenant governor under newly-elected Governor Butch Otter, and that's how he came to be the keynote speaker for all of us serving as lieutenant governors.

Yet I paid no mind to his admonition that lieutenant governors had to stand ready to step up as governor should the incumbent governor leave or step down. I thought that this sort of thing might happen in Idaho but it didn't happen in New York, California, Illinois, Florida, Texas, and Massachusetts, the major states of the Union in terms of political influence. I listened respectfully to Lieutenant Governor Risch of Idaho but pretty much knew his advice would never apply to me.

Talk about conspiracies of improbability, I did take a commitment at that lieutenant governor's conference to host the following year's conference for the organization in Buffalo, New York, where I would be, by then, improbably enough, governor of New York. I was asked to speak and told the assembled that I thought sessions among lieutenant governors would be better spent in training on how to bring down an airplane in flight, or how to put sugar in a car engine, or how to perform a fake Heimlich maneuver in a restaurant: "Oh, I'm squeezing the governor, I'm squeezing the governor. Oh, look at that, the governor didn't make it. What a shame, now I'm the governor."

Despite all this lighthearted mirth, I did take my job as lieutenant governor seriously, did work very hard at doing it well, and was, as ever, willing to take the governor's place at the family planning event that morning. I was already invited to speak there but pretended to the governor's office that I was going to put something together quickly, though I had already rehearsed my remarks. I complied with the request, gave the keynote speech, took a few questions from the media, and returned to my office somewhere around noon. I then sat at my desk and had a conversation that lasted 35–40 minutes with an old friend, not really noticing that not very much was going on around me. I didn't notice how eerily quiet it was. I was just like one of those leading characters in a movie where the audience knows what's going on but the leading character has no idea what's about to happen and then, all of a sudden, he's dead.

I then got a second request around 12:30 PM and this was absolutely bizarre. It came from Charles O'Byrne, my chief of staff who, if I thought about it, knew better. I knew that he knew better but I didn't think why he would know better. He said over the phone that New York's cardinal, Cardinal Edward Eagan, would be meeting with the governor at 1:30 PM and that His Eminence was bringing all the bishops from the state with him. Here was the kicker: the governor had not yet arrived in Albany and wouldn't be able to attend such a meeting and so it was suggested that I go and have the meeting in place of the governor. This was a different magnitude of a request from just pinch-hitting for the governor at a family planning event.

Charles O'Byrne had been a priest for seventeen years and not only knew the significance of the cardinal but knew government very well. So he knew that this request was for a head-of-state to a head-of-state meeting. It was as if the Queen of England had come to the United States to meet with then-president George W. Bush, and President Bush sent Dick Cheney instead. Then again, In the case of Dubya and Cheney, it might have been appropriate. But, with Cardinal Egan and Governor Spitzer, it was simply something not done by the governor of the state to the state's most important religious leader. You cannot delegate a head-of-state to a head-of-state meeting to someone who's not a head-of-state.

I explained this to Charles, who then said, "Well, look, they gave it to us, why don't you just take it?"

"Have you gone crazy? You know protocol as well as I do."

When met with his silence, I added: "The minute I walk into the room, the cardinal or someone on his behalf is going to let us know how inappropriate this is and how the governor should be present at the meeting." Surprised that O'Byrne would even try to get me to attend the meeting, I got off the phone and had my lunch brought in by my assistant and secretary, Narda Singh.

At about five minutes to one, I got a message from O'Byrne that the governor's secretary, Richard Baum, would like to talk to him and me on a conference call in a few minutes. Again, I was surprised that the secretary wanted to talk to me and to my chief of staff rather than talking to me alone, and I was now beginning to think that everybody had gone crazy in Albany that day.

That was the understatement of the year and a prelude to hysteria as I had never witnessed it in my life.

IT WAS 1:05 PM when the call came in and Richard Baum seemed to be whispering. I would learn six months later, when I had a conversation with him, that the reason he was whispering was that he was in the bathroom of Governor Elliot Spitzer's apartment on Fifth Avenue in New York. Spitzer had learned that he had been caught in a prostitution sting case and was preparing to resign at 2:15 PM. Baum was telling him repeatedly that, "We have to call the lieutenant governor." But Spitzer stalled, saying, "We'll call him, we'll call him." We were now an hour and ten minutes away from this historic event.

Baum urged Spitzer one more time, "Why don't you call the lieutenant governor and let him know what's going on?"

Spitzer replied, "Don't worry about him, we'll type something up for him to read." Baum knew I couldn't read anything that was typed, particularly on that short notice. I needed time for memorization. Equally, he knew that I sure couldn't come up with seat-of-the-pants responses in such a dramatic situation. Above all, Baum realized that the first thing I was going to ask him when I became governor was, "Why didn't you tell me?" because by then he'd be *my* secretary. So, his strategy was simple. He called up and got Charles O'Byrne and myself on the phone and attempted to tell me about this: I got the gist of it but I couldn't hear every word he was saying because he was whispering, something about a prostitution ring and Governor Spitzer's being caught up in it. I thought maybe it was an investment club and somebody invested in an illicit prostitution service, but that turned out to be woefully wrong. This phone call was absolutely shocking, maybe the most shocking call I ever got, or ever will get, in my life.

Finally, I said to Baum, "Well, it sounds like the governor is in a big mess."

"The governor is finished, he's going to resign at 2:15."

I said, "What time is it now?"

He said, "1:15."

After this phone call Charles O'Byrne came up to my office and even I could see he was as red as a beet.

I said, "Charles, what do you think I should be doing now?"

"I think you should write down a few notes, which we will call an inauguration speech."

As O'Byrne exited, I found myself standing in the middle of my office, a beautiful office—the lieutenant governor's is the most beautiful office in the entire building, the entire capital. It's so gorgeous that the first time Governor Spitzer came to see me there, he joked about the office and said, "Want to trade?" Going along with his joke, I shot back immediately, "Governor, it's the only thing I have. Let me keep it." He and I laughed but the joke shows how impressive the lieutenant governor's office is. Imagine this: Its ceiling is 37 and a half feet off the floor; there are bare brick and ornate glass, skillfully etched; there is beautiful architecture, columns and pillars, there is even leather upholstery on parts of the walls, but I couldn't see any of it right then because I'm blown away by what O'Byrne has just told me. I am in a trance, bemoaning the fate of Governor Spitzer, whom I considered to be a great friend, and his family as well, whom I found to be totally lovely, all of them, and that's when the immensity of trying to take his place and think of what to say within the hour struck me hard.

I collected myself quickly, contemplating whether I should talk to one of two people first, my wife Michelle or my father Basil Paterson, former deputy mayor to Mayor Koch, former secretary of state under Governor Cary, first African American vice-chair of the Democratic National Committee, and a renowned mentor and thinker among many national leaders. I decided to call my father first because maybe he could help me with my wife. I called my mother to ask her if she knew where he was and, as luck would have it, he was home that day. She put him on the phone and I proceeded to tell him the details of the last 15 minutes of my life. He was undoubtedly shocked, but when I asked, "What do you think I should be doing right now?" it was amazing how quickly and precisely he provided instruction.

"Do the other state leaders know about this, David?"

"No. I just think Governor Spitzer and his staff and maybe some family members know about it but the word has not gotten out yet, no media reports are even suggesting anything is different than an ordinary Monday in Albany."

My dad simply repeated the question: "Do the other state leaders know about this?"

"I assume not."

"You need to tell them."

"Well, I think the governor would like to tell them."

My father almost laughed, then stated flatly: "He hasn't even talked to you, David, but guess what? When you become governor in less than an hour, the first thing they're all going to ask you is, 'Why didn't you tell me about this?'"

Thereupon he proceeds to list the state leaders:

The senior United States senator for New York, Charles Schumer.

The junior United States senator for New York, Hillary Clinton, then campaigning for president in a tough primary against Senator Barack Obama of Illinois.

Attorney General Andrew Cuomo, former Secretary of Housing under President Clinton.

Comptroller Thomas Denapoli, former Assemblyman voted in as comptroller a year prior.

And Charles B. Rangel, the dean of the delegation and the congressman from Harlem.

My Dad parenthetically reminded me that Rangel had been very ill recently and wondered if I knew that. I affirmed that I did. He said he had seen Rangel the day before and that Rangel seemed to have had an epiphany during the time he was ill. He came very close to death and was now planning his life and what he really wanted to accomplish in the time remaining to him in Congress.

Listening to my father's reminiscence of the Rangel encounter was frustrating me to no end. I'm looking at a red dot against a white background on my watch, which was a second hand for people who are legally blind but have some vision. As I'm watching the dot go around the clock I'm completely aware that precious time is flying by, being squandered. This is an issue my dad and I have had my whole life. His mind was so quick and his thoughts so concise that he could flip from one discussion into another at a moment's notice, so I might call him up and say, "Hey, Dad, I'm coming down with something. I feel sick and dizzy and think I might have caught the flu." He might then say, "Oh, that's really bad. Oh, by the way, can you believe the Jets lost that game on *Monday Night Football?*"

We were having another one of those moments right now, but I considered it the most inopportune time for this digression and decided if that dot goes around one time, meaning one full minute had passed during what I saw as an unrelated story, considering what's going on in my life right then, I'm going to react. The red dot goes around, completing a full minute, and I screamed into the phone, "DAD!"

And he says, "What?"

"Focus!"

"On What?"

"On what the heck we're talking about right now!"

Hanging up, he and I ended that conversion for the moment, but I'm agitated that some of the time was wasted. Yet I don't waste any more time over spilled milk. Instead, I called my wife Michelle, but she doesn't get any of the preamble my dad got, all she got was, "Michelle, Elliot Spitzer got caught with a prostitute. He's going to resign in 50 minutes. And that will make me governor."

Michelle paused and said, "Wow, David, is that true?" and I said, "No, Michelle, it's an early April Fool's joke! Of course, it's true!" And then I continued to complain.

Michelle said to me, "Ah, David, are you feeling a little frustrated right now?"

Slowly, holding my tongue, I said, "A little frustrated? I just have to make an inauguration speech in less than fifty minutes and I haven't the slightest idea what to tell New Yorkers. I haven't even heard from the governor so I don't even know how to characterize this situation."

And then I heard Michelle say, "Well, you know, David, I have never really told you this, but I consider you to be the most resilient person I know. Whatever happens, no matter how much you're beaten down, no matter how much you're disenchanted, no matter how many times I've seen you mistreated, you somehow pull yourself together and respond with grace and class. So you may be feeling frustrated right now but myself, as a voter, as a New Yorker, I think you're the right person to be sitting in that seat right now. You may be frustrated but you're the right person to address this situation. How can I help you?"

Either I felt like shedding a tear or I shed a few. I couldn't believe that such an encouraging and wonderful thing had been said to me right in the middle of this mess. Instantly my emotional mood shifted from frustrated to decisive, to actually deciding that I was not going to let Michelle down or any other New Yorker down. I said to myself: *I am ready and I will rely on instinct, I will rely on decorum, and I will rely on honesty, and take New Yorkers through what was going to be a very difficult time.*

I acted on my father's advice to call the other state officers about 15 minutes after he proposed it. My first return call arrived at about 1:30 PM, it was from the one I would have least expected to hear back from so quickly. Hillary Clinton had just won the Texas and Ohio primaries the previous Tuesday, but the gap in the delegate count with Senator Obama seemed insurmountable so she was hard at work trying to pull out this victory. Yet she did return my call almost immediately.

"David?" she asked, "there was something about your message that makes me think that something is wrong."

"Senator, It appears that in about half an hour I will be sworn in as governor."

"OH MY GOD, what has happened?"

"No, Senator, it's alright, the governor's health is fine but he is going to resign within the hour."

Senator Clinton paused and said, "Well, what is the reason causing him to resign?"

I started to speak and then held my breath because I thought, *How do you explain a sex scandal to Hillary Clinton?*

So in a voice that quaked with anxiety, I responded, "Well, um, he, well: he was caught with a prostitute."

Thinking the connection may have broken down, I made a remark to see if she was still there. I said, "You know, a prostitute, did you hear that?"

There was another long pause of silence until the senator finally broke it with a comment, "Oh, what a world!"

She then comforted me, saying that I might feel a sense of anxiety that events were moving too quickly, but to please relax and realize that she was with me and that the president was with me and that they would be good support because there is nothing that I could go through that they hadn't already been through. Prophetic words indeed, as it turns out.

And I felt relieved

I WAS INFORMED that the minority leader of the Senate, Malcolm Smith, and the first deputy secretary to the governor, Shawn Patrick Maloney, had joined Charles O'Byrne outside my office for a 1:40 meeting. It was now 35 minutes to the moment. Do I tell them, I wondered? I knew O'Byrne knew what was going on, and I would later find out that they all knew what was going on, so we were all pretending to each other that we were all keeping a secret that we all knew. The only person who didn't know what's really going on was me; the emperor had no clothes. Again, It's like being the protagonist in a movie where everyone knows what's going on except the protagonist.

At ten minutes to two, I got a phone call from my secretary, Narda Singh, informing me that there was a *New York Times* story on the wire that Governor Spitzer was going to resign at 2:15, so I tell Shawn Maloney and Malcolm Smith what was going on and they acted surprised, though they knew all along. Spitzer came on the TV screen at 2:15, or perhaps a little later, with his wife Silda at his side, who appeared to be chagrined by all the happenings, and the governor said that there was a personal matter that he had to attend to, and that he hadn't decided what he was going to do, and that he would get back to the media later. Of course, this only fanned the fire and by three o'clock this crisis had become critical.

I gathered a couple of my assistants and told the state trooper who drove me that we were going to my house. I thought this would be the best option since I didn't really know what was going on, still hadn't heard from Spitzer, and I thought it best to stay out of sight rather than being confronted by television cameras, flashing lightbulbs, and a bunch of probing questions that I couldn't possibly answer. So, I went go back to my house in Guilderland, 17 miles west of Albany, and waited there so that I wouldn't do anything or say anything that influenced the process.

I opened my office door to leave and fifteen camera flashes popped. I closed the door, faced my secretary Narda, and said, "I think my life just changed." Now I am forced back into my office. I got on the phone and spoke to the staffers of the state Senate administration, the people who run the building. They informed me that they know a secret way out of the capitol that I never knew about, and that this secret exit can actually be accessed from the lieutenant governor's office.

During this time, I also got a call from the assembly minority leader, Jim Tedesco, who said, "What's going on?"

"I really don't know."

He said, "But listen, you and I have worked together, we've both been minority leaders, you're now lieutenant governor and I'm minority Republican leader of the Senate. So, I would assume that if you become governor, we'll have a very good working relationship."

"Absolutely, Jim, I couldn't think of any other relationship we would have."

I got off the phone. Five minutes later Tedesco had told the AP that I was taking over as governor, I had acknowledged it to him, and said I'd be happy to work with him. This prompted a call from Spitzer's office asking what the hell was I doing. This would be the first of a plethora of self-serving pariahs—and other members of the chordate family—who would invade my life in the coming weeks.

I realized then and would realize in the days to come, that this international scandal would also be like a sequel to the movie *Invasion of the Body Snatchers*. It appeared that everyone around me was going crazy; even my most trusted aides were doing these really wild and strange things. Friends of mine were overreacting. People were calling me on the phone, people who had no real relationship to politics, and then calling back two hours later saying, "I called you, why didn't you have the decency to call me back?" Somebody mentioned that the Albany District Attorney, David Soares, was investigating Governor Spitzer over an accusation that he'd used the state police to follow the majority leader of the Senate, Joe Bruno. This caller suggested that I should get a look at that investigation; later in the conversation, apparently after I said, "Yes I probably should get a look at the investigation report somewhere down the road," the caller went to the district attorney's office and asked him to hand over the report of the investigation so far.

Of course, the district attorney flew into a rage and, not wanting to contact me directly, contacted the Comptroller Tom Denapoli. In turn, Denapoli came to my house and admonished me that the district attorney didn't like me interfering with his investigation. I sent back an apology saying I didn't interfere, that I had just mentioned to somebody, that yes, I would probably like to ask the district attorney about the investigation at some point. That's when the person I mentioned this to took the law and the investigation into his own hands. I managed to stomp this fire out just in time for another to flare up, one that had followed me home to Guilderland with the state trooper, my five assistants, and the hordes of media now camped outside the house on my lawn.

WHEN I ARRIVED at the house about 5:30, my aides and I barricaded ourselves in and ordered food to try and stay out of the action. An African American union leader named Norman Seabrook had seen Denapoli coming to my house on national television, coming in and then leaving, and Seabrook called the comptroller of the city of New York, Bill Thompson, to let him know that he had tried to reach me three times and that I had let the white man in the house but didn't talk to him. This was the second fire I managed to tamp down with a few soothing words. Meanwhile, one of my assistants had a gentleman friend who was interested in her but was ten times more interested in coming to the house and seeing me about his clients. He was a lobbyist. Why? I wondered, would he think I'd be interested in talking to him, or to his clients, in the middle of this circus?

By Monday night the crisis had mushroomed into worldwide breaking news. Governor Spitzer was being referred to as "client number 9," which was apparently how he was described by the service providing him with a prostitute. Two hours later an amateur guitarist went viral on the Internet singing the song *Love Client Number Nine*, an adaptation of the song *Love Potion Number Nine* by The Searchers. This started a trend. The next day people all over were singing the lyrics to this adaptation.

While this farce whirled around me I sent a staffer out to a restaurant on Route 20 to get us some takeout food. There was simply no way that I could go outside without being besieged by the hordes of media surrounding the house. When the staffer returned with comfort food, I sat and ate with my five staff members while we continued to monitor all the cable and network news, plus all the gossip being disseminated on the Internet and through texting. These five staffers were Shammeik Barat, Echo Cartwright, Sarah Lewis, Jeffrey Pearlman, and David Johnson. I'll always remember the comfort they tried to give me in this moment of absolute horror, during which I had spoken to Governor Spitzer for a little over a minute.

That conversation occurred about 4:30 PM and lasted just over a minute. The governor told me, "I haven't decided what I'm going to do yet, but I'll let you know."

This was not a big help.

I WOKE ON the morning of Tuesday, March 11, with the thought that maybe this was all a dream; maybe this didn't happen. But as I started to draw the shade in my room I heard the voices, "He's up, he's moving" and next I heard cameras whirring as they were trying to take pictures of me in my PJ's through the window. National media had by now formed a ring around my house, and they were trying to figure out what was going on behind the green door. This had been the title of a famous seventies porn movie, *Behind the Green Door*. In my case, the green door was appropriate because my wife Michelle had painted the front door to our house lime green. I liked it, but apparently not too many other people did, and it became an interesting discussion point for a couple of days as the media held a vigil outside my house.

Even from outside the house the media members would actually talk to me using the television as an electronic lobbyist. CNN reps on camera were saying, "Lieutenant Governor, we know you're in there, why don't you just come out and say hello. The country doesn't really know you, so we'd really like you to just come out and say hello." This was said with fake innocence, as if, should I have come out and said hello, they weren't going to blast me with any questions; you know, they said just come on out and we'll have a nice front lawn chat, like an old FDR fireside chat on the radio. Yeah, right! I felt like the perpetrator in a hostage situation, listening to the great Sidney Poitier's dulcet tones in *A Patch of Blue*: "Come on out, we're going to take care of you, just come out of the house." This was gently pleaded like they weren't going to machine-gun me with questions once they lured me onto the lawn.

The final indignity occurred when Charles O'Byrne called me that morning at home. He'd been out in a bar the night before with several staff members and everybody was in a frenzied state, frenetically talking about all the possibilities now that it appeared Spitzer would have to resign. According to O'Byrne, the secretary of State, whose name was Lorraine Cortez Vasquez, came over to him and, in front of a number of witnesses, admonished him that just because the governor resigns, does not make the lieutenant governor his replacement, that in fact the secretary of state has to certify that the lieutenant governor is who he is and is duly qualified and therefore is certified to become governor.

But Secretary Vasquez's pronouncement that evening was that she would not certify David Paterson as governor until she had a meeting with the lieutenant governor. Presumably, this was a threat that there would be no certification unless the secretary of state was able to exact some political patronage, some political favors, or some position in exchange for delivering the certification. O'Byrne informed me that he'd like to schedule the meeting for that afternoon so, as he put, we could "just get it over with."

"*Au contraire,*" I responded, "tell the secretary of state that the world is watching and if she doesn't want to certify that I am now the governor she can explain her decision to the media and to the rest of the world. And, in addition, please remind her that in a change of government all of the major officials in an administration tender their resignations and I can't wait to accept hers."

Charles was startled, "You really want me to tell her that?"

"I hope you remember what I said because I'm not going to repeat it."

O'Byrne must have completed the task exquisitely because, by the end of the day, two of Vasquez's strong supporters were calling to tell me how abusive O'Byrne had been to the secretary. This unparalleled fracas was ended following a meeting between Roberto Ramirez, the former Assemblyman and county leader of the Bronx, and a very strong supporter of Vasquez, and myself. My father, Basil Paterson, also put in a very good word about Lorraine Cortez Vasquez.

Subsequently, she was fiercely loyal to me the whole time I was governor. This was so much so that at one point, when I was going to choose a lieutenant governor, I would have taken Lorraine and tried to make her the first Hispanic lieutenant governor of New York.

When I presented her with the possible opportunity, she thought it wiser to pick an unaffiliated, apolitical civic leader which would be better should there be a court challenge. We agreed that was the right course but, had I run for re-election to the office of governor, I would have asked her to run with me. So why did this professional woman, who I had worked with all this time and never had a problem with, engage in such an outburst as O'Byrne described? I believe that the tectonic eruption of instability arising from the story about Spitzer and its worldwide publicity, including the paradoxical conflict with his reputation as "the sheriff of Wall Street" and a squeaky clean prosecutor, sent the entire Albany institution of state government into hopeless freefall, with even my closest friends and associates caught up in an orgy of cannibalism, seeking power, resources, and recognition.

ALTHOUGH I DIDN'T know this at the time, the speaker of the New York state assembly, Sheldon Silver, told me later that, by the day after the story broke, Spitzer was already changing his mind: he was not going to resign, he's was going to go to counseling and believed by doing this he would be able to diminish the story, absorb some responsibility, and move on with his term as governor. At some point on Tuesday afternoon, or into Tuesday evening, according to Speaker Silver, Spitzer called to tell him there was a move afoot in the assembly to try to impeach him and he would like to have it quashed. Speaker Silver responded that he could hold the assembly off for about a week, but that's it. Spitzer countered: "But you're the speaker, you can stop it whenever you feel like it." Silver replied softly, "Governor, you don't have a vote in the house." By saying this, Silver was informing Spitzer that he didn't even have Silver's vote.

Silver told me all this about two months later, on a June evening as we sat up late chatting in the governor's office. It was about 11:30 in the evening, just the two of us talking. The story fascinated me, naturally. Silver said that when he informed Governor Spitzer that he didn't have a chance of continuing in office, instead of Spitzer getting upset, the governor simply stated that Silver's negative response was what he thought it would be, but that Spitzer's father mistakenly believed that Silver, as Speaker and head of the assembly, could stop the impeachment movement.

In any event, I was informed at my house on Tuesday night, March 11th, that Governor Spitzer would resign at noon the next day. I made a determination at that point: I didn't want to look weak, alone, or unprepared when he did resign. I didn't want to be standing in Albany, by myself, being sworn in with just a handful of friends and family members and whichever legislators hadn't already left Albany because the session for that week ended in a matter of hours, on Wednesday morning. So I asked my counsel, who was formerly Governor Spitzer's counsel, David Nocenti, to contact Governor Spitzer's lawyer, the noted and renowned attorney Ted Wells, and request that Governor Spitzer make his resignation effective on the next day that the legislature would be in session: Monday, March 17, 2008. My request was honored and that would be the day I would be sworn in. The resignation took effect at one o'clock and we planned my inauguration this way so that I might have a little more time to put together my rough "notes" that Charles O'Byrne referred to as my inauguration speech.

ON MONDAY MORNING, March 17, 2008, as I was coming out of the shower, I learned from Charles O'Byrne that I had a call already. He informed me that President Bush would be calling in five minutes. I hurried to get dressed; for some reason, I wanted to be dressed when the President called me: I had never talked to a President on the phone before and thought that I should be prepared and decorous. O'Byrne also pointed out that, overnight, the federal reserve had taken measures to prevent the collapse of Bear Sterns, the investment bank, and, as a result, my staff wanted to change two or three paragraphs in my inauguration speech, which had only been completed the day before. I had stayed up all night trying to memorize it. That my daughter had to be taken to the hospital in the middle of that same night only added greater stress to the situation: Ashley had a stomach ailment after her sudden return from the trip to Aruba with her friends.

As O'Byrne and the speechwriters were inserting new material into my inauguration speech for me to memorize in the next couple of hours, I got another phone call and I'm asked to hold for President Bush. About twenty seconds later this man comes on the phone and says:

"Hey, how you doing up there?"

"I'm doing alright!"

"My people tell me you're gonna do a great job."

"Well, Mr. President, with all due respect, sir, your people have been wrong before."

He laughed and I thought to myself, *This isn't President Bush, this is my staff playing a joke on me, because this man can't be President Bush.*

And then the president said, "By the way, how do you like New York's executive mansion?"

"Well, I've only been on the first floor, the public part. I haven't been in the living quarters."

"Trust me, you're gonna love the living quarters," he said and proceeded to describe them to me. He described the guest room and mentioned that he's the only president who's stayed in the New York executive mansion and that I'll see his name prominently displayed in the guestbook. Now, it's undoubtedly true that this is President Bush and, oh my God, I had almost made a nasty remark like Annette Benning in the movie *The American President*, when she thinks that the phone call she gets from the president, played by Michael Douglas, is a joke being perpetrated by someone else. Boy, am I glad I didn't say anything like that to President Bush.

We talked for about ten more minutes and he couldn't have been more supportive and more engaging. Congressman Charles Rangel told me once that he had worked with presidents going all the way back to Nixon and that his favorite one to interact and try to conduct business with was President George W. Bush. And that day I found out why so many people appreciated him.

The next thing I knew the state police took me to the capitol where I came into the governor's office for the first time since the last time I had visited Governor Spitzer. It was eerie to be in that office and now be in charge. But the pains of probable lapses in judgment by people all around me continued to distract me from my mission. A trusted friend had arranged an interview with a reporter who said he was going to "off the record" help me, and I told him a few personal items that he was about to write in a news article, which is the last way I would have wanted any personal information to come out right after my inauguration speech. Yet, out of loyalty to my trusted friend, I had gone along with this unnecessary interview.

Another very notable New Yorker, who had served in government, had blown up my phone for three days until I finally agreed to meet with him, whereupon he let me know that Governor Spitzer intended to give him a prominent position in the state in June and therefore he now wanted to know if I would respect the appointment. I told him that I would respect the appointment, that I thought it was great. But then I got a phone call from the individual who currently held that post, telling me that he had no idea that his term was ending in June and that a poll of the Spitzer hierarchy showed that none of them did either. So the whole thing was a scam and an attempted shakedown.

Meanwhile, somebody was perpetuating the rumor that my nephew, my brother's son, was my illegitimate child. At the time the boy was born, his mother had been living with my brother for two years, where everyone saw them living together, where everyone knew, before the boy's birth, that his mother was pregnant by my brother—well, the story now is that it's actually my baby and "they"—whoever "they" are—had covered it up for me. Mercifully, this idiocy was only a minor inconvenience. To show

how crazy people get, including members of the media—maybe especially members of the media—this attempt at character assassination ran in *New York* magazine, where even a quick vetting by editorial and legal would have revealed its falsehood. Then again, in print media, circulation is king.

This is how loony everything surrounding me became. Farce is only fun in the theater, not in real life, especially when you're at the center of it.

By 11:00 AM of inauguration day, I had a massive headache to go along with my other problems. That's when I got a visit from the mayor of New York City, Michael Bloomberg. When I started to tell him about these problems, he said, "Why don't you just sit on the couch, lean back, and get some rest. I have some business to do myself. I'll just sit in here and conduct my business and as long as I'm in here no one will come in and you can actually get some rest and pull yourself together."

That was the most magnanimous gesture I had received in the last week. I just kind of sat there and closed my eyes. I didn't think about very much. I entered a kind of meditative state and, within about half an hour, I was ready to take the mantle of responsibility from Governor Spitzer.

Before I knew it, it was one o'clock and I was standing in the chamber next to chief judge of the court of appeals, the late judge Judith Kaye, who would swear me in. She was among the most gracious and considerate people, among the very few I ever had the pleasure to interact with. Right before the inauguration ceremony, in a low voice, my father said to me, "In spite of the suddenness of the circumstances, there is no other governor I have worked with that was any more prepared or able to manage the affairs of the state than you are." My mother—who was singularly most responsible for my ability to be one of the first blind students to go to public school, who heroically managed my life when I got out of high school in three years, who helped me through very difficult times when I was in college and in law school, and who had always pushed me to greater heights—didn't seem to react to this sudden event other than just to be supportive and to have a mild sense of humor about the whole thing.

My then-wife Michelle read me a very sincere and warm congratulatory email that she had received from the former first lady of New York, Silda Spitzer, one that made us both cry, and while Michelle enjoyed that her husband was becoming governor, she had great sympathy for the Spitzer family's plight. Then again, my daughter Ashley, recovered from her stomach ailment, seemed poised and ready to take over as press secretary, secretary to the governor, or maybe go on the court of appeals if necessary— whatever.

My son, Alexander Paterson, Alex as we know him, did not seem as excited as everyone else. Somehow, he seemed to know that his plight over the next few years would be far more difficult than that of the rest of us because he had no protection as the rest of us did. Attending middle school at the Booker T. Washington School at 108th Street and Columbus Ave, he, as Spitzer's children had been before him, was now being followed every-where he went. Sometimes, especially when he was eating somewhere with friends, someone would come over and ask him a question; on one occasion, right before he answered the question he remembered he had seen a *Daily News* press sticker on the window of the car and declined to answer the question.

Another time when he was in a pizza parlor, he took issue with what he thought was an extra charge on the bill. While the restaurant owner and he were talking about it, one of his friends said, "You better not bother this guy, his father will close this place down." The restaurant owner went to the school, not to complain about the kid that said it, but, totally unfairly, to complain that Alex had not stopped the kid from saying it. So, clearly Alex had the most difficult burden, and the reality of it was dawning on him much sooner than on the rest of us. He understood it fast. But he has always had an almost sensory ability to glean what is happening before it does.

RIGHT BEFORE I was sworn in, Sheldon Silver removed a glass from the lec-tern, saying he didn't want me to knock it over and distract from the pro-ceedings. I immediately changed his remarks by saying that he did not want me to turn the inauguration into a Jewish wedding by breaking the glass. I then told the assembled and the world that I had taken a DNA test about three weeks before; one of Albany's public broadcast stations had asked me to participate in an experiment that had been conducted on the PBS series *African Lives*, where they took DNA tests of prominent cultural and civic leaders in the African American community to determine what African countries their blood was indigenous to and where any white blood may have been traced. As it turned out, my test luckily showed 42 percent Irish and, of course, this was Saint Patrick's Day, so I wore a green tie and bid everyone a happy Saint Patrick's Day from one of Saint Patrick's little known descendants. Both the joke about the speaker not wanting me to break the glass and the joke about the DNA test were designed to calm the audience down, to try to bring some order and humor to what had been such a hysterical situation for the past week.

I then outlined the difficult task we would face with two crises occurring simultaneously in the state, one the leadership crisis caused by the sudden vacating of his position by the former governor, the other an economic crisis that was at our doorstep since New York derived most of its revenues from Wall Street firms, some of which were then going down the tubes, one having been saved only the night before. I continued to outline my vision for the state: principally, firming up education and healthcare while eradicating poor housing, substance abuse, crime, unemployment, and inadequate facilities for schools and hospitals. Then I went against the advice of my staff and speechwriters by making a statement I'd heard somewhere before, I wasn't sure where. I simply said, "Permit me to reintroduce myself, I'm David Paterson, Governor of the State of New York."

Thunderous applause followed and a resonating flurry of enthusiasm rippled through the audience. I must admit that not all of the positivity was because I had become governor; much of it was that Elliot Spitzer was no longer governor. Nonetheless, I had attended inaugurations for governors going back to Governor Cary in 1978, when my father was sworn in as secretary of state, and, not to be immodest, I was thrilled and humbled by the response of the attendees at mine.

My overriding thought about Spitzer's departure and my elevation to the role of governor is that it's the best benefit I ever got from sex—and I wasn't even there.

Now, SPEAKING OF governors.

Saturday, February 21, 2009:

The national governor's association, which is an organization of the Republican and Democratic Governors from all fifty states, is held in Washington DC almost annually. It includes a meeting with the president, some selected presentations by different cabinet members, and a dinner on Sunday night at the White House with the president and the first lady. There are also seminars held by different governors and I attended one held on Saturday afternoon involving the environment where the co-hosts were governor Arnold Schwarzenegger of California and Governor John Corzine of New Jersey. I arrived at about 20 minutes to four and was making conversation with some other early comers when Governor Corzine asked to have a word with me. He shared that he had a very important meeting that he had to attend, and he'd like me to take his place co-hosting this colloquium. My immediate thought that I shared with him is that I'm completely unprepared to host such a conference.

"Oh, don't worry about it, Governor," he said. "These seminars are really hosted by one governor, and in this case it's Governor Schwarzenegger of California, but what we do, so it doesn't become partisan, is we have a member of the other party side there. Which is all I was really going to do. Governor Schwarzenegger is going to run the show. All you really have to do is introduce yourself, and he'll take it from there."

Still not convinced that this would be the entire responsibility, I accepted it and Governor Corzine left the room. At about five minutes to four, I started to wonder where Governor Schwarzenegger might be. As to this point, I was yet to meet him. At 4 o'clock, members of his staff identified themselves to me and said, "Governor Schwarzenegger is running late, let's start the program." I alerted them to the fact that I was not supposed to be the cohost, that Governor Corzine was, but he's left, and I don't have the slightest idea who's speaking on the program. They said "Oh that's alright we have the list right here" and that's when I knew this was not going to end well.

For the next 75 minutes of this 90-minute seminar I sat there trying to remember the other names of the panelists that had only been read to me once, elicited from one guest what her role in the administration was only to be admonished as she's Lisa Jackson, Head of the Environmental Protection Agency, took commands from Governor Schwarzenegger's staff out loud so the whole room could hear it and I must say that I didn't really mind being the puppet it's just that when they let the strings show it's very embarrassing.

It was now 4:45 PM and the sun was setting, as was my credibility. Finally, at about 5:13, only 17 minutes before this inexorable meeting was about to end, who bounced into the room but Governor Schwarzenegger. When he's informed of the fact that I was forced to host the event without any previous preparation and the fact that I couldn't read the schedule of the topics to be discussed, he sat down, sheepishly leaned forward, and in his inimitable way said, "I am so soary."

This is when I learned that, an icon, a person that you have the most profound respect for, not only because of his acting career, but how seamlessly he entered government and found some great issues to champion, when they've put you in a situation such as this, you can humanize them instantly, as I did, when I looked right back at him and said, "You are soary alright." But this only evoked laughter from the governor, who put his arm around me and extolled my virtues to the audience and had them applaud for the fact that I had tried to do my best to govern, if you will, this unwieldy process.

A year later when I attended the national governor's association again, and everybody was attacking me, telling me I should be resigning—the victim of fake news x 10 and much of it emanating from former friends—it was soothing to be the beneficiary of a very supportive quote that came from Governor Schwarzenegger. Later in the year, he invited me to one of his environmental conferences in October of 2010 and I even went shopping for ties with him during those few days. *Tie shopping with Arnold* could be a TV series. Like *Celebrities In Cars Getting Coffee*, but with ex-governors.

Arnold, like all of us at some point, has had some of his own tribulations but I just remember the interesting conversations we used to have and how gracious he was to me.

2

What Do You Mean I'm Blind?

I started out as a child. I was raised at 370 Grand Avenue in Brooklyn, New York. I was born in St. John's Hospital, now known as Interfaith, and my first challenge was actually not my vision. Apparently, I didn't even know if I had a vision problem. When I was three and a half years old my brother, whom I had heard was born, was going to be brought home today and my grandfather suggested to me that my grandmother, my father, and other family members should go to the hospital to bring the baby and his mother home. He also suggested that we might shovel the snow off the sidewalk to make it easier for them to walk in when they arrive, but when it came time to do so, he couldn't find his shovel. At this point, my grandfather became irate about a guy named Steve. He seemed to say that Steve had taken his shovel and when he caught up with him he was going to do something to him. He was not happy. He knocked on some of the neighbors' doors but no one was home. We went back inside and he served me lunch, I was playing on the floor with my toys, he was eating some lima beans and probably had an early cocktail out of his frustration with this guy Steve who stole his shovel. As the afternoon went on he was very nice to me but still grumbling about Steve. I remember when my parents came in, they always say that the father carries the baby so that the other child won't be jealous. I was just surprised that the baby, my brother Daniel, had hair and he didn't look to me like he was just born.

Anyway, I thought that it was interesting about this guy Steve and I didn't forget about it and about two years later when I was about five or six I asked my grandfather about Steve and he didn't really remember the situation too well and he didn't know too many people named Steve and he didn't think any of them had his shovel. So, I might have asked him again about it over the years. When I was twelve my grandfather passed away and we were sitting around the house in mourning and his relatives from North

Carolina had come and there were a lot of family members there. Again I raised this issue about Steve and nobody knew what I was talking about. So, I thought I would wait until sometime after he passed and so about a year later when I was thirteen years old, I asked my grandmother about Steve, she didn't remember anyone on the block that lived there named Steve. So through the years it was just in the back of my mind, I never really thought about it and then, when I was thirty-three years old and my grandmother had passed away, we buried her and shortly afterward I said to my mother one last time, "Mom, you lived in that house when you were growing up, why was he complaining about this guy Steve taking his shovel?" My mother thought about it and then she appeared to have an epiphany and she said "No, David he didn't say that Steve took his shovel, thieves took his shovel and you didn't understand what he said," and I realized, like a lot of things in life, sometimes it takes years, sometimes thirty of them, for us to realize what's going on around us.

I don't know when I realized I had a vision problem but I think I was about five or six. I was going somewhere with my friends David Samuel and Johnny Young and they kept asking why I was always looking down. There might have been a cousin of David's, Mark Glover, who asked me that question because it seemed that David and Johnny seemed to recognize I needed help sometimes but never really said anything to me about it. It was people I'd just met who always seemed to have a reaction, rarely positive, to my disability.

It is alleged that something happened to me when I was three months old, like an ear infection, and that led to the eyesight condition that I have. Many doctors who have examined me have confirmed there's no way that could have happened, however, it still appears on websites about myself and I guess at this age there's no sense in trying to fight it. I'm just going to have to live with that story. But the reality is that optic atrophy, which is scarred tissue that lies between the retina and the optic nerve, impairs the eye from transmitting the vision to the retina from the optic nerve, and in doing that has left me with no apparent vision in my left eye. I can see my hand when I'm waving it in front of my left eye and I do have light perception there and I can see something because once when I was injured and had to wear a patch over my left eye, I realized things were coming up more quickly on the left than they had before so there's some vision there but I hardly think it's measurable. The vision in my right eye was measured at 20 over 368 which I think has diminished since then, but it left me with two basic sight problems. Nearsightedness to the extreme, and that you're only seeing out of one eye, so there are problems with depth perception. This would dictate and pervade the entire movement of my life.

I must have been fifty years old before I realized that when I dream, I dream exactly as I see, so I'm walking down the street in the dream but I can't read the signs. Now it's my dream, I think the signs should be much bigger since I'm running the show, not the government, but that's not the way it is. My dreams reflect the same incapacity that I have in wakefulness. Even when I daydream it's always out of the right eye, it's as if my left eye doesn't exist.

That old saying that people with a disability make up for it with their other abilities, I think it's not true. I don't have a particularly good sense of taste, I don't have a particularly good sense of smell, I probably do rely on my hearing far more than other people do—although, I'm not planning on starting a career in piano tuning—but I don't think it's any better than anyone else's, and my sense of touch, I would say, is normal to below normal. I don't recognize faces particularly well. I tend to recognize people whose appearance is a little exaggerated. If they're very tall, heavy, if they have something interesting about the way they wear their hair, it makes it easier for me to observe them.

My lack of facial recognition is exemplified by an incident where I was taken to dinner by a very nice young woman whom I'd gotten into the law school she was now attending. Forgetting that people who are twenty-four or twenty-five years of age have a different way of dressing than those who are nearly thirty-five years older, I determined that I would take her to a restaurant—very popular in Harlem—known as the Red Rooster. Also, a place where I probably know half the people in the restaurant. So, when she comes in wearing a very short hot dress in the middle of December, everyone notices me sitting with her. A woman comes over and says "Hi David how are you?" I said, "Nice to meet you." She says, "Nice to meet you? I was married to you for twenty years." This is a clear example of why I don't recognize facial expressions, but I didn't need to see Michelle's face to know the expression she must have had about this woman in this really hot dress who looked like she was a third of my own age.

So, I asked her what brought her to the restaurant. She said it was Denise's sixtieth birthday. Denise Ellis is the Godmother to our son, Alex. I know her very well, so if they're celebrating her birthday, five or six of Michelle's friends must be sitting over there chattering about how I'm in this restaurant with this woman who looks thirty-five years younger than myself, so when the dinner was over I walked over to the table and I brought the woman—who's actually the daughter of a woman I went to law school with, named Lynn—and I said, "Michelle, you remember Lynn don't you?"

She took another look at the woman and I could tell she immediately said you must be Lynn's daughter. She said, "Yes I am, I'm thanking the governor for getting me into law school." As we walked away, I ran back to the table and said; "ladies, I'm leaving the building now, you'll have to find something else to gossip about." Through the uproarious laughter, I was able to govern the surroundings even though my lack of visual acuity caused it in the first place.

All in all, I perceive myself as blind. Not partially blind, not legally blind. Whenever you're not able to see something, you're blind. There's a point behind every driver's shoulder called the blind spot. It's the spot the driver can't recognize oncoming traffic, even if the driver recognizes it a little it's not enough to prevent an accident. So, I acknowledge people with severe eye difficulties as blind, and I see myself as one of them. I'm not better than anyone because I have some vision, I don't think anyone is worse off than me whether they have more or less vision. But, there certainly was some kind of public policy that existed when I was a child to try to humanize blindness. In other words, to try and make blind people seem like everyone else. That's what the itinerant teachers would tell my classroom teacher when I went to public school. "He's just like everyone else." I'm not just like everyone else. The lack of vision creates a different culture. You perceive the world through a different prism. You evaluate yourself much differently than others do.

For that reason, the biggest mistake that was made in my early education, in spite of the superhuman and valiant efforts of my mother, is that I should have learned braille. But they weren't teaching braille that much anymore. They thought they could just use large print books and they didn't think the students would go much beyond high school so it didn't matter. Whatever the reason, there certainly was an attempt to diminish the social effect of people with some sight, being compared with the blind or even being treated as if the problem was that difficult to live with, when in fact, the lack of accuracy-of-assessment for people like myself, caused all of us serious problems in the educational system.

Years later in 2009, I would offer a state of the state address to the legislature and the citizens of New York state. I did it without a note, I also did it with the flu. Although I was widely congratulated for being able to memorize over an hour's worth of the speech, probably sixty hours to memorize this information, deprived me of time that I needed to devote to other issues such as selecting a United States senator. That whole issue blew up in my face later on because I didn't pay enough attention to it and the people who were supposed to, were lax in their duties. If I'd have been able to read braille, I could have practiced the speech using the braille. Perhaps not at the same speed as a sighted person but still allowing enough time to serve other duties simultaneously.

The New York City public school system would not guarantee my parents that I would always be in the class with sighted students. My mother always explained to me, "whoever you go to school with is going to be who you socialize with and who you'll do business with." And, "if you are separated into a different category with people who have the same problems you do, you're going to have a pronounced disadvantage when trying to compete in the workplace." I think that most educators at the time didn't think that blind people would be in the workplace, and they were right because there is still a 68 percent unemployment rate for blind people in this country. This is a dismaying fact when you consider the educational productivity of the blind is 3 percent higher than the national average. So we've been able to educate blind people along with other disabled, but we haven't been able to employ people because we haven't put the same effort into the workplace that we did into the schoolhouse for those who need the assistance the most.

So here I was in September 1959, standing in front of Marshalls school in Hempstead New York. My parents had gone to Westchester, they had gone to other parts of Long Island, and had even considered out-of-state venues to make sure I was in a public school with other students. The Hempstead public system was probably one of the top three systems in the state. They had already sent blind students through their school system and could accommodate me if the family would move to Long Island. My father was trying to start a political career in New York City at the time but he got moved to Hempstead—along with my brother Daniel and myself—so you could tell who was running the show in this relationship.

A fly in the ointment arose when Mrs. Stein, my kindergarten teacher, asked my mother in front of her friend Billie Allen and myself, to take David home and give me a week to settle down the class and then bring him in. My mother thereupon said, "so in other words, my son has to be marked absent for 5 days while you get control of the class?"

Billie said, "I'm a teacher myself and I can get control of the class in 20 minutes with David in the class if you'd like to watch."

I didn't hear this repartee between my mother and the teacher. Billie Allen, a noted actress who lived in Hempstead with her family at the time, told me about this years later. Apparently, this feud escalated to the principal's office and fifteen minutes later I was placed in the class with the rest of the students.

Mrs. Stein couldn't stand me for the whole year. She once confined me to the bathroom for two hours because I couldn't wash finger paint off my fingers fast enough, but I was in the class and cooperated, as did all the other students. I could write notes on loose-leaf like all the other students. I could draw pictures in art class like all the other students. But I couldn't read regular size print for more than a few minutes without my eyes hurting terribly and I couldn't see the blackboard at school. So, my education was a game of hopscotch where sometimes I was sighted and sometimes I was blind. This was never quite resolved until much later in my life when I took the series 7 and series 63 exams to get my license as a registered financial advisor. The problem was enhanced by my absolute disdain for being referred to as blind or in any way impaired. Unfortunately, this was a result of the edict of the time that you'd be a whole lot better if people said you were normal. When someone said I was cross-eyed, I was quite indignant.

This may sound strange, but whoever you are, and whatever you are, you should be proud of it. If you're proud to be black, if you're proud to be a woman, if you're proud to be an American, if you're proud to be a New Yorker, you should be proud to be blind. Even though it causes you problems, it's who you are. It's what you are. The question is, what will you be? And you'll never be anything until you resolve the fact that God created you the way you are and even if there are imperfections, this is who you are.

If I could have an operation right now to have my sight restored, the only reason I would do it is that it would be an adventure. It would be interesting to see what the world sees, what I've missed all this time. Maybe even at this point, I could try out and play for an NBA basketball team. But failing that, blindness has afforded me an immense opportunity.

When I used to sit in school and guest speakers came to address us, they always seemed so perfect and they always acted as if they were perfect and were admonishing us to be the same. When I went to see people as a state senator, and even before when I went to schools to talk about different issues, they knew I wasn't perfect from the minute I got there. This gave me an innate opportunity to communicate with people. Not from the top down, but from person to person. I would tell young people, *I know you have problems, I have problems myself, you can just look at the way I tried to get on this stage, you know I have problems. So don't look at me as some state senator who was a straight-A-student, always successful in romance, and always makes a lot of money. I'm not that person. I'm closer to you than any of your teachers.* With this positioning, I would get respect—or *street cred* as they say—and was able to impart to some of these young people, experiences that they probably wouldn't have listened to otherwise.

So, in many ways, I have used my own inadequacies to forge relationships with individuals who are probably, at times, so hurt and so turned off that they don't think they would be noticed by anyone who's that important. I know, I've been there. You have to generate trust from your lack of importance, the lack of the fact that you might be a governor, the lack of the fact that you might have been successful in business after serving the people, and that's often the way to engender cooperation.

I saw the movie *Moonlight*, and in the movie, it's just horrible, the bullying, and the vicious way that a child who is smaller or a little different, is treated by other children. I experienced that same treatment. There was a scene in that movie that was acted out in my own life and I couldn't believe it. If there weren't witnesses I don't think you would believe it. You'd just think I put it in the book after seeing the movie. But I've talked about this for years. I was on the playground and this kid was picking on me and he pushed me down. When I got back up and tried to fight him, the other kids held me back and he said "Yeah hold him back before I knock his other eye out," and he walked away. I then went to his classroom, there were two third grades, he was in the other third grade. I went in the classroom and hit him in the face with my lunchbox, and my lunchbox wasn't the lunchbox kids use today, it was metal, and after a while, the ends were jagged which had now cut this kid's face. He got sent to the principal's office and I was restricted from going on the playground for a month. When I finally got out from this punishment—to my absolute surprise—nobody messed with me because they thought this was a guy who will come in and hit you with a jagged steel lunchbox when you least expect it. We shan't mess with him.

IN 1998, TWO years after the passing of my late friend Lacey Johnson, I went with his wife Cathy to his son's school. His son was being bullied. He has a communication disability. Years later Walter would go on to serve in the US Navy. He was one of the greatest achievers I've ever met in my life but at the age of eleven, he was being picked on, ridiculed, and sometimes assaulted by the other students. Finally, he got mad and punched somebody in the class-room. Both students were sent to the dean of students and to their guidance counselor to be admonished. The parents were supposed to come to the school and I decided to come along with Cathy. I thought Lacey would want me to do that. In the meeting when they were talking about how they won't allow any violence, I pointed out to them "You won't allow violence but you'll allow bullying all day and somebody can't take it anymore, they turn around and hit somebody. And I don't see why they should be blamed." I proceeded to tell my story and the dean of students said; "Senator, are you condoning violence?" I said to the Dean, "No, but at times, it sure can be helpful."

The damage that bullying does to the self-esteem of victims has, until recently, gone unaddressed. The afflicted don't strike out against their abus-ers, they become more and more isolated, losing self-esteem, and we now observe, many of them take their own lives. As I matured I rejected the notion that one has to be the direct recipient of pain to appreciate such injustice. I admired the white men and women who left their safe commu-nities to join the civil rights movement, such as Father Iakovos, the leader of the Greek Orthodox church, whose picture may be found on the famous *Life* magazine cover, joined by Martin Luther King Jr. and three other civil rights leaders prior to the march on Selma, Alabama in 1965. I befriended Father Iakovos prior to his passing in 2005, and learned how he worked to combat hatred around the world. I longed to demonstrate my condemna-tion of mistreatment of others beyond my own backyard. Experiencing racial discrimination by other blind people and denied employment due to my disability, from black people, as I saw it, placed me in a universal vantage point as an observer.

In the past, I saw the placement in this position as being very negative, feeling shunned by almost everybody, but now I was embracing a unique combination of experiences that would guide me in an effort to ignite change. Being black and blind, I wanted to be in charge of bringing a voice to the needs of these and other disparaged communities. I saw a venue to raise the quality of health care, education, affordable housing, and the cre-ation of jobs for those who had the ability but lacked the opportunity. That place was called public service.

To ROUND THIS out, I'd like to share a story from my early years that may help me to bring you into my world and better prepare you for what ensues.

April 29, 1980:

I was in my third year at Hofstra law school which would, unfortunately, not be my last. I was studying for an exam that was scheduled for the next day around 3:30 in the afternoon. I could hear the distant rumbling of a car with no muffler which I knew belonged to my dear friend Lacey Johnson. He was probably coming over to see if I needed any help or to take me to lunch, but I was so engrossed in the issues of family law that I decided not to answer the door when he arrived because I didn't want any interruption. I took a break at about 4:00 PM when New York's first news station, 1010 WINS, reported the death of Alfred Hitchcock. Oddly enough, I was contemplating some of the works of Hitchcock like his TV show *Hitchcock Presents*, his movies; *The Birds, North by Northwest*, and my favorite, *Rebecca*. In this movie, the leading character, played by the actress Joan Fontaine, is never addressed by her first name, a subtle way of demonstrating her invisibility to all around her. Unbeknownst to me, in the next couple of minutes, I'd be wishing I was invisible.

The front doorbell of my house rang, again I decide to ignore the invitation and go back to my studies, but on the eighth count of my doorbell ringing, I surmised, Lacey—or whomever—knew I was in the house, so I threw on my jeans and sneakers to answer the bell. After the thirteenth ring, I started down the stairs and there was a pause, making me think the person was leaving. I was halfway down the stairs when there was a thunderous admission as someone—or someones—smashed in the front door, breaking the lock and scaring the living daylights out of me. I retreated to the upstairs bedroom to call 911, forgetting that I'm standing right next to a panic button that would turn the alarm on. It sounded like the intruder was coming up the stairs, the same direction to which I must run to a window from which I'd like to escape. I had jumped from this site twelve years before. There was a pitched roof which prevented me from falling straight down and it turned me upside down, breaking my wrist on arrival. I got into the room steps ahead of my pursuer, shut the door, opened the window, knocked out the screen, and jumped out of the window horizontally, going over the barrier and landing on a cement surface that we used to play basketball on and had erected only a few years before.

Invigorated by my triumph I want to get out on the street where people could see me before my pursuer(s) could catch me. Running past the side

door, the intruder came out at the same time but didn't see me. I couldn't
stop, so I ran right over the intruder at which point, I deduce, but have
never been positive, that there are two of them. I ran as fast as I could across
the street to elude them, not even looking, I ran on to the entrance of the
Hempstead State Parkway. I wanted to cross the bridge into Rockville
Center to Mercy hospital which was a venue where I thought I could seek
help and call the police. Running across the bridge on the sidewalk, I realized the perpetrators could see me from the front of my house, and who
knows, might shoot me; so I decided to get down and crawl across the bridge
which would protect me from any gunfire. Still moving quickly, bent over
on my hands and knees and sometimes my feet, I ran into a nun who I know
is probably leaving after finishing her shift at the hospital.

"May I help you, young man?" she gently inquired.

"I'm just trying to get to the hospital." I told her, "because I think somebody may be trying to kill me."

Clearly not convinced of the authenticity of my remarks, she smiled and
said, "Well, have a nice day and a nice trip to the hospital."

So, I get to the hospital, call the police, walk back over the bridge, and
was probably about 100 yards from the house when the police showed up
and grabbed me. I compelled to them that I am the resident of the home
who called them in the first place. They ask me if I can prove I'm the resident of the home and I conjecture as to how I might do that?

"Do you have a picture of yourself in the home?"

"I have whole albums in the home and we can look at them while these
people are getting away!"

So, in the end, the perpetrators were never really found, they didn't get
anything, except for knocking over my plant which I'm still mad about. I
learned how to jump out of a window without having to go to the hospital
and was reminded that if I had answered the door to Lacey when he came
by in the first place none of this may have happened.

I'D LIKE TO share one more story about the difficulties relating to sight, dating, and transportation. A little story I like to refer to as " The Blind Date
From Hell."

Tuesday, April 17, 1984:

A woman named Diane Matthews, who had been my secretary when I
worked for the NAACP for about a year prior to finishing law school, told
me that I would be perfect for her friend Connie. So, I agreed to meet

Connie in front of Hunter College where she was taking graduate courses and I took her to a popular restaurant on 94th and Columbus. The restaurant was known as Under the Stairs. This was the first time the two of us met each other and, in the end, it truly would be, in more ways than I would ever know, a blind date.

I had a feeling that things would not go well, when 20 minutes into the date while eating salad, and not remembering where I had just placed the salt, I felt around the table with my hands to retrieve it. Connie found the salt and handed it to me, which I thought would be the end of the dilemma. Until Connie asked this rather probative question, "Why did you not ask me for the salt?" I had to think about it but gave an answer as honestly as I could, that I knew the salt was on the table, if I didn't know there was any salt at all I might have asked her, but I just had it and accidentally misplaced it. Her summary judgment was that; *I have trouble asking other people for assistance*, which happened to be true, but I didn't want to be invaded in this space so early in our interaction. I also became keenly aware that her graduate coursework was in sociology and, apparently, I had an amateur psychiatrist as an escort that evening.

As the evening progressed, I made some comment about my brother Daniel, whereupon I was confronted with the fact—that I had known my whole life—that my brother has total vision and I have very little of it, therefore; I must have some resentment against him because of this circumstance. Over dinner, she continued to inform me that I must have some hostility towards my parents because they pushed me by mainstreaming me into education and society before I was properly equipped for it.

All I knew is that I just wanted to get the check and put this woman in a cab and not have any further sessions with her while living on the planet earth. The fact that she claimed she was only interested in men who were 6 feet tall and above, gave me an out. Or so I thought. Since her class didn't end until 8:30, it was already late in the evening when we started this dinner so she requested that I accompany her home to make sure she got there alright. By this time, it was 11 o'clock. I was annoyed. After some negotiation, I agreed to ride the IRT number 3 train to its last stop, which, at that time, was New Lots Avenue, where we caught a taxi and dropped her off where she lived in East New York. There was a barrier in the taxi that made it hard to communicate with the driver so I asked her upon her exit to tell him to take me to the Long Island Railroad station at Atlantic Ave. Once again, she let me know that the closest train station was at East New York and I firmly instructed her that I wanted to go to Atlantic Ave because at this hour it would be difficult to get a train from the place she was suggesting.

When the taxi driver arrived at the train station, I had a feeling I had arrived at the wrong place and I should have asked which station it was but he said, you're at the train, walk straight. I walked straight and realized now that I was at the East New York train station, in probably one of the worst neighborhoods in the city and on the first warm night of spring. I am now standing on the platform of the East New York train station waiting for the Long Island Railroad. Within fifteen minutes it comes but this feeling of relief is vanquished as the train goes through the station without stopping. This is because so few people get on or off the train at this late hour, that the train runs right through and this is what I feared when I asked Connie to send me to Atlantic Ave, which was the terminal. After two other trains followed suit by not stopping at this station, I came down the stairs deciding to walk around and find help. All I heard were a bunch of young people interacting in ways to which I did not want to become a party, so I went back up the stairs. Mind you, I was wearing a three-piece suit, carrying a briefcase, and felt like I was wearing a sign on me that said "has money, easy to mug." This time I walked down the track and saw what appeared to be another opportunity for escape. A pay phone in the subway, I walked over and picked it up and assessed that someone had cut the insides out of the phone. I resolved that I would now have to sit in the station until 5 o'clock in the morning when another train might stop but that was four and a half hours away.

While I sat, hoping no one on the street knew what easy prey was available by climbing the stairs to the train tracks, at about 2:20 am, I saw a train. It was not going to Long Island where I was going but heading to Brooklyn on the other side of the tracks. Unlike the other trains, this train didn't seem to be moving as quickly and I realized that this train, for whatever reason, was going to stop at the station but was on the other side of the track. I grabbed my briefcase and, as fast as I could, ran down the stairs, under the tracks, and up the other side.

There was someone else in the subway. I don't know if they were waiting for a train or just standing around homeless, but I ran over them and I, to this day, pray that they are in good health, but I had no time and was in fear for my life. I ran upstairs and heard the bell that signaled the doors closing on the railroad. Diving into the air, I thought, if I could just get between the doors it would stop them closing but I got completely through, landing on the floor as the doors closed. Another passenger got up from his seat and yelled "Safe," while making the sign as would an umpire after someone dove into Home Plate.

I rode the Long Island Railroad back into Brooklyn, which is the terminal at Atlantic Ave, and took a train to Rockville center, then took a taxi to Mercy hospital where I had gone to report the burglary of my home, walked across the bridge, and arrived home at five minutes to 4:00 am on April 18, a Thursday. Recounting this story to my boss at the DA's office, Al Annenberg, at 9:15 the next morning, I was invited to stay home that day, providing any future first dates had to be approved by the office, namely him.

Around 12:15 in the afternoon I got a call from Connie who wondered why, when she called the DA's office that morning, I wasn't there. I more than let her know how insensitive it was for her to demand to be escorted home, how it made it impossible for me to get home at a decent hour, and that by sending me to the wrong train station—even after being advised it was the wrong station—she endangered my life and guaranteed that I would never want to interact with her again. Her response was that she could have gotten home by herself but she wanted to teach me a lesson which was that I extend myself too much and tried to do things beyond my ability in a hopeless attempt to negate the self-realization that I actually have a severe disability.

The late judge Dwayne Hart, who attended Columbia University with me and also served with me in the Queens District Attorney's office, told me that if anything like that ever happened again, to please call him. I suggested to him that I would have called him that night but there was no phone available. But he was with me in 1985 at the swearing-in of a wonderful Judge, Wayne Scarborough, who also died much too young of an aneurysm. At the reception, Dwayne and I were greeted by none other than Connie, who wanted to say hello. At the same time, she said hello, I felt pressure on my right arm, completely immobilizing my ability to move it and then my left arm, later Dwayne said to me, "It was the only time I've ever seen you so agitated that you might become violent." I don't think I felt that way at all, but we'll leave the Freudians to determine whether Connie's method of ingratiating herself with me by telling me what's wrong with me, is an effective dating practice.

WELL OK, PERHAPS just one more story before the big story unfolds. I wanted to include this one because, no matter what injustices or indiscretions I was accused of, I think this one speaks to the boundary of any lack of integrity I may be accused of.

Did I ever cheat? Well, there was this one time:

I will not mention venue, the time, or the institution, other than to say, it was obviously an educational forum and an administrator who always seemed to have it in for me. She always resented when I seemed to ask for special assistance in situations where my disability prevented me from learning but she exceeded herself this time by forcing me to take an exam for a class I had never attended. I had registered for the class but had turned in a change of program card which was either misplaced or abandoned.

"You are taking this class." She demanded.

"The exam is in three days, how can I take an exam for a class I didn't attend?"

"You can ask the person that taught the class I was sitting in whether I was there or not and that's the exam that's appropriate."

I got the institutional response about how this is on the program card and that's the exam I'm taking. With the distinct advantage of hindsight, going to the administration would have been a far more valid activity than the one that I performed but I think I was so badgered and belea-guered by the negative responses I was getting from this institution that I just decided that I had to take the exam. A dear friend of mine had recorded his notes from the class but it was almost thirteen hours of read-ing time and was arduous at best. I showed up at the exam on the appointed day, took the exam, and got a B. This is the story of how I did it.

I modeled my actions after Richard Wright, who, in the book *Black Boy*, said that he stole from grocery stores and other places to get the money to leave the south and relocate to Chicago in his early life. He later wrote that he didn't think that was thievery because he never took anything from anyone before or since, however, he thought it was a payback of how the institution of the United States Government had stolen so many opportu-nities from him. This might be a weak excuse and it probably is, but this is how I surmised that it would be fair play for me to cheat on this exam, especially since it affected the time of my graduation, which I could not have done, had I not passed this course. The exam was recorded on tape, so I came to the exam in a room that was being guarded like Fort Knox and listened to the questions. Unbeknownst to the examiners, I was recording the questions on a Dictaphone that accompanied me to the exam room. I then feebly started trying to answer the questions having read very little of the course and knowing this grade I would get, if I had to hand in this compilation, would be a G. Then, at the appointed hour, I retired to the men's room, reached under the stall and handed the Dictaphone to my chilly homeboy, the oldest friend I had, the person I knew three weeks after I was born; as he was born to my mother's best friend. We'll just call him PC. He came to the school acting as if he was waiting for somebody and went into the men's room prior to me so that if anyone was following me they wouldn't see him come in after me. He left the school and drove ten minutes away to hand the tape to a friend of mine who we will refer to as G. G had taken the class the previous semester and he believed he did well enough in the class the pass the exam even though it had been 6 months since he took the course. He dictated the answers, handed them back to PC who met me during another bathroom break. I was so nervous I dropped the tape and was reminded that I'd dropped every pass he ever threw to me while playing basketball. I scurried back to the exam room and fiercely copied everything I heard on the tape onto the exam notebook and handed in the exam. Failing to pick up my diploma at graduation, I came a couple of days later and was greeted by the administrator. "Please come in and sit down," she said. But as soon as she got the door closed, her jubilance turned to scorn and she said:

"I know you cheated on that exam."

My answer was, "I know I did not do that."

We did a round of "Yes you did," "No, I di-ent" moments.

She then said "Look, I have your diploma here, and I'm going to give it to you, the issue is, I don't know how you did it. We watched you every second of the time you were there. We watched you through the window when you didn't know we were there, and we watched you outside the men's room. I need to know this so I can stop anyone else who tries to do what you did. "Come, do me that favor."

"Why would I do you any favors when you would have me take an exam that you knew was almost impossible for me to prepare for?"

"Well, that's how I know you cheated because it was impossible for anyone to learn that amount of material in two and a half days."

"Well," I retorted, "I shouldn't have been taking the exam, I should have been taking the exam of the class which I actually attended."

The argument continued until I said, "If you say one more thing to me, I'm going to the administration and I'm going to complain about you."

A few years later, someone did, and the administrator was suspended for a while by the school, but after this threat, she withdrew her complaints and handed me my diploma. She even said "Congratulations." As I was walking out of the room and opened the door to walk out, she said, "I will say one thing, you are a very clever individual." I went through the door, leaned back, looked at her, which was the last time I would ever see her, and said, "That's what they tell me."

3

The Name I Will Never Forget

Friday, May 20, 1983:

It's my birthday. I'm completing the sixth week of my service in the Queens District Attorney's office. I did not have a license to practice law in New York but I was a candidate for admission, meaning I was taking the bar exam and awaiting results. In that role, I could practice law under the supervision of an attorney. Those of us in my situation were allowed to practice law as if we were licensed attorneys, with the exception of trying cases in the Supreme Court and putting cases into a grand jury. At that point, I was working in the forensic bureau of the DA's offices where we handled cases that involved a mental disease or disability suffered by the defendant. The best-known type of forensic case would be the insanity plea. After would-be President Reagan assassin John Hinckley, Jr., pled not guilty by reason of insanity, the insanity defense proliferated in popularity to the point where states had to set up special bureaus in their prosecutors' offices to deal with it. This is what New York had done and that is what the forensic bureau in the Queens DA's office dealt with almost exclusively.

In New York, the insanity defense is called the "not responsible plea." It cuts two ways: if a defendant is so bereft of his or her ability to help their lawyer at trial because of their mental disability, that defendant cannot be tried at all and would need to have their trial put off pending further psychiatric care and evaluation. Mike Cavanagh, who was hired by the Queens DA's office and put in the forensic bureau the same day I was, had already tried some cases and conducted some hearings to determine whether a particular defendant was fit to go to trial. Prior to coming to the DA's office, Mike had worked for a defense attorney, so it was no surprise that he was put right into the courtroom. He would eventually rise to the highest levels in the office.

As I entered the office on the third floor of the Supreme Court Building on Queens Boulevard, I didn't realize that I was about to get a birthday surprise, an event that would become a legend in the Queens courthouse to this day. I was greeted by my boss, Alfred Annenberg, the chief of the forensic bureau, who said to me, "Happy birthday." My first thought was, "Who squealed?" Before I could review the list of probable culprits, Annenberg said to me, "What would you like to do for your birthday?" and I responded, "Well, maybe after work we'll all have a drink." Annenberg retorted, "You have a drink on all your birthdays, I'm talking about doing something on your birthday that you've never done before." He smiled and said, "Tell me something you've never done that you'd really like to do."

I told Annenberg that I could think of a few things but I wasn't telling him any of them.

He said, "Why don't you take a case into court?"

I said right back to him, "Why don't I not take a case to court and we'll say that I did."

He said, "No, seriously, this isn't difficult, this defendant is very bereft of his faculties and the psychiatrists agree he cannot help his lawyer at all. All we need you to do is get up and explain that to the judge. The defense also agrees that the defendant is mentally ill and thereupon, he'll be sent on what is called an order of retention to a psychiatric facility where he'll stay for one year and then he'll be reexamined. And he'll stay there forever unless at some point he's determined to be mentally able to stand trial. All you have to do is take the case in, make that statement—it's all set up—and then we'll go out for drinks for your birthday."

I said, "Okay Al, I'll do it."

And then he said, "You know I think people would want to remember your first day acting as a lawyer, so I've invited a few people to come and watch, even a couple of people I know in the office who happen to be friends of yours. I think that will be a lot of fun and then we'll take them out for drinks." Of course, when he said "friends of mine," what he actually meant was just all the black people in the office.

And I'm thinking, *Oh My God, I'm going to be so nervous and then there'll be people who know me sitting there watching, also a courtroom full of people who don't know who I am: this just sounds like a recipe for disaster.*

But nonetheless I go into court that afternoon, the case is called, and I get up and say, "I am ADA (meaning Assistant District Attorney) David Paterson appearing on behalf of the Queens District Attorney's office."

I paused for a second and took a deep breath. "Your honor, in the case of the state versus Ronald Galella." (Parenthetically: five minutes before my death, I may not remember who I am but I will remember the name, Ronald Galella.) I resumed my spiel: "Two court-appointed psychiatrists have both arrived at the conclusion that Ronald Galella suffers from a mental disease or disability that makes it impossible for him to assist his attorney in his own defense and therefore, under the law, we submit that he be placed in a psychiatric facility for a period of one year, under an order of retention, at which time he'll be reexamined by a psychiatrist to determine if his condition has improved enough to be tried for his offense."

Wow! I nailed it. I was pleased and quite relieved that I'd been able to perform my duty this afternoon. There was a great defense attorney who specialized in "fitness to proceed" cases, Victor Scavullo, who was the brother of photographer Francis Scavullo, and quite a gentleman. I don't recall whether he was the defense attorney on this case but he might well have been. At any rate, whoever it was, said, "Your Honor, we concur with the prosecutor's assertions."

And had he stopped right there I wouldn't be telling you this story over thirty years later. But he added: "Mr. Galella has written a letter to his Honor and he would like the judge to read this letter. After the judge has read his letter he will comply with whatever decision the judge makes."

And so the letter was passed from the defense attorney to the court clerk, who passed it along to the judge. The judge reviewed it and handed it back to the court clerk, who in turn handed it back to the defense attorney. I was now becoming anxious because one thing I had learned in my six weeks in the DA's office was that if one side of the case and also the judge see something, then the other side should see it as well. I had seen Al Annenberg ream out lawyers for allowing the defense, and the judge, to talk or to exchange information and then not demand that we the people see it as well.

So, I stepped a little closer to the bench and said to the court clerk, "I'd like to take a look at that letter."

He looks at me like I'm from Mars, and says, "YOU want to read the letter?"

No doubt my blindness was known throughout the courthouse. But Annenberg had another admonition for those of us that worked for him. It was not to let the judges, and certainly not the opposing attorneys, and especially not the court clerks, push us around; Annenberg taught us to go at them hard. This was not my nature but I knew that this was the first time

I had appeared in front of a judge and I didn't want to get off to a bad start with my boss. So I said to the clerk, whose first name was Frank and I don't think I ever knew his last name, "I speak English and I assume you do as well. So, yes, I'd like to see that letter, and I'd like to see it now." Reluctantly the clerk retrieved the letter from the defense attorney and handed it to me in a hostile manner.

I took the letter and held it up. Now I knew that I couldn't read this letter, but I believed that no one in the room really knew how much I saw and how much I didn't see, so I held it about two inches away from my eyes, where if I had glasses on I probably could've read it just a little but I just started moving the letter as if I was reading it and thinking now I've accomplished my purpose. At a certain point the clerk touched the top of the letter with his hand, trying to take it away from me, and I pulled it down to my side and looked, as well as I could, right at him and said, "I'm not finished reading this letter."

He responded, "well, we've got a lot of cases to do today."

"You're the one holding up the process because as soon as I finish reading this letter, you can get onto the other cases," I snapped back.

Confident I had put the clerk in his place I held the letter back up and resumed my imitation of reading the letter. But in the background, I started to sense a murmur and began to feel something had gone terribly wrong. I just heard all of this chatter and then an attorney named Leonard Livote, who's been a friend to this day, someone who I appointed to the Supreme Court twenty-seven years later as governor, said something that I'll remember for the rest of my life. He whispered, "David, please give them back the letter. Mr. Galella is insane. He didn't even write a letter, he just wrote the letter G on the page, and just kept writing G's up and down the page. For the last two and half minutes you've been reading a page full of G's and the lawyers behind you can see it."

Now shocked, and also in an elevated stage of embarrassment, I handed the letter, with my fingers trembling, back to the clerk, who had his arms folded and was even more hostile than he was before. Then the Judge, Judge Seymour Rotker, a renowned legal thinker and tireless worker, peered down from his vantage point and said, "The only thing I find more profound than this letter is the prosecutor's appreciation of it," which sent the courtroom into uproarious laughter.

Rooted to the spot by embarrassment, I fantasized back to the perils of the cowardly lion when he appeared before the Wizard of Oz and became so unraveled that he ran out of the wizard's chambers and dived through a window. I would have gladly done that if such an egress were available. I came out of the courtroom trembling in fear at what Annenberg was going to say. But, after putting his arm around me, Annenberg said, "Listen, I sent you in there to get a defendant sent to a psychiatric facility and that got done, now let's go have drinks."

I wish I could end the story here but, after about three vodkas, Annenberg broke into hysterical guffawing, remembering the judge's quote, and blurting out: "Paterson is pretending he's reading a letter and all he's doing is staring at a page full of G's . . . G-G-G-G-G-G-G-G up and down the page, and he's just holding his own. That's the funniest thing I've seen in thirty years as a lawyer."

Of course, there is one other name that I'll never forget. And that name is Glover.

October 21, 1975:

It is my first day at work for the Municipal Credit Union. It was the credit union for the city and state employees but it was not connected with city or state government. I had worked for my father in the summer of 1974 and that was a great experience, but this was my first new job, new bosses, with a bunch of people I'd never met before. It was in this role that I would meet one of the most dynamic people, who was funny, creative, and interesting, and his name was Alan.

Alan had served time for possession of drugs and was now trying to rehabilitate himself. I was starting a job, pursuant to Professor Basil Rout's request, that I find a job before returning to Columbia University. Also working at the credit union was a man named Glover, who was about thirty years old, a very nice looking gentleman, must have weighed close to three hundred pounds, was very bright, and never wasted a moment in telling us how bright he was.

There was a fiscal crisis in New York City in 2005, and on the first of July many New York City employees were laid off. When we, working for the credit union, called to ask how they were going to pay their loans back, some got very irate because they thought we were the city's agency and wanted to know how *you could expect me to pay back the loan when you took my job away from me?* Nonetheless, we would pursue them as we were directed.

On one occasion, a woman came down to refinance her loan and was greeted by Mr. Glover. He had a different greeting than one a member of the credit union might expect. His greeting was, "Hello I'm Mr. Glover, take off the G and we're in business." Following the refinancing of her loan and her resistance to invitations from Mr. Glover, she reported this to human resources. Glover's denial that he had spoken to her in this way might have had some meaning had not another woman, standing behind her in line, chosen to come with her and be a witness to the event.

Glover got into some trouble and I never knew what the trouble was, certainly not the trouble he would have gotten in had he done something like this in modern times. But his real problem was that we haunted him with this instance almost every day.

So, for example, when he got a phone call, a woman named Bertha Virgil, who went on to be an outstanding union leader, would introduce the call by saying "Mr. Glover, take off the G and we're in business, on line 5." About a year and a half later, in May of 1977, I took the day off to visit the Dean's office at Hofstra Law School to discuss how I might find people to read to me and ways to tape classes pursuant to my acceptance to Hofstra Law school.

When I arrived at my desk at Municipal Credit Union the next day, I was greeted by two older gentlemen, both of whom were mentors to me, and both have long since passed away, Ben Cochrane, and Lloyd Brown. I thought they were fighting back tears, but they were fighting back uproarious laughter as they regaled to me how Glover's ex-wife had charged into the office the day before with all three of his young children and said, "Glover if you're not going to pay child support for these kids you can take care of them yourself." Whereupon she took a metal file basket and, like a frisbee, flung it across the room forcing Glover to dive for cover. Take off the "c" and it's over.

By the end of the day, I counted seventeen individuals wanting to recount their version of the story to me. Whenever there's an office place incident, you can go home and tell your families, but your families don't know the people who work there, and they really aren't familiar with why the situation would be so interesting. But a co-worker who wasn't present when the incident occurred was the prime candidate for endless retellings of the story.

With the children running around screaming and Mrs. Glover hurling a second object at her divorced husband, the human resources director, Lillian Wade, bounced out of her office to inform Mrs. Glover, if she didn't leave, the police would soon be called. Her request was answered by a stapler traveling at major league pitchers speed, missing Ms. Wada's head by inches, and driving her back into her office never to return.

As employees in the office tried to take the children out of the way, the melee continued with Mrs. Glover hurling phones, typewriters, and anything she could get her hands on. Her tirade carried her to the employees' lounge where she grabbed a small television that management had put in so that employees could watch a little television while they ate lunch. But now the little television itself was airborne and would have broken but not for a diving catch performed by a messenger named Willie Johnson. Later that day, I asked Willie why he risked his health diving on the floor to catch this television, and he said, "Had she broken that television and the ladies here couldn't watch *All My Children* during lunch, they would have murdered her."

According to my friend Alan, the rampage ended with Glover hiding in the locked men's room while his former wife stood outside the door, as Alan put it, huffing and puffing like the Big Bad Wolf ready to blow the house down.

The incident was very sad in that this woman, who was just trying to take care of her children after her husband left, wasn't getting the help she deserved, and I would surmise not getting enough help from the courts. The frustration spilled over and manifested itself in this very ugly incident, but something about Glover being on the other end of it was just apropos for the—at times—condescending way he treated employees. The sad part about it for me was my friend Alan left the credit union around the same time I did and never really caught on with any other companies, slipped back into his addictions, and at some point, actually became homeless.

Seventeen years later, my assistant Anna Barrow, was assisting me at the supermarket near my building on 132nd Street and Malcolm X Boulevard. A man came up and tried to talk to me but his speech was so muffled that I couldn't understand what he was saying. Anna intervened, physically moving and backing the man up away from me and giving him her card so that he could contact her and she would help him with whatever his problem was. But he said something and when I asked him to repeat it, he said, "It's Alan."

This was the last time I ever met him. I couldn't believe how unkind the years had been to him. He was with some woman and they were about $20 short for their purchase—according to the cashier—so I motioned to the cashier to let them go through and I would pay their bill along with mine.

Well, this did not go over well with Anna, to whom I didn't have time to explain the closeness of this friendship years before. Alan was clearly elated, and he thanked me, even though I would not have been able to recognize him in that condition. And so, as we parted for the last time, I said, "Hey Alan, what do you remember about Municipal Credit Union?" and somehow, Alan stood up straight, his eyes seemed to clear, a smile came across his face and he said, "Glover, take off the G and we're in business." Alan and I hugged, and I never saw him again.

I HAD ANOTHER run-in with a court officer and Al Annenberg later in my career. On that morning Annenberg and I went into the courtroom in the Queens criminal court. We were standing at the prosecutor's table when Annenberg saw the court officer coming in and instructed me to go and ask him what time they're going to call our case. Annenberg went and sat on the bench and I walked up to the court officer and, before I could speak, he said to me "Go sit down and wait for your lawyer."

I responded; "But, sir."

"*But* nothing, go sit down . . . or your lawyer will be picking you up in the pens."

The pens ware the criminal court's equivalent to the time-out chair. In other words, if a lawyer was held in contempt of court or a defendant was acting up too much, the court officials would put them there until such time as they had calmed down and were ready to conduct themselves properly in the courtroom.

Feeling diminished, I went and sat on the bench next to Annenberg, who said to me in a voice much louder than the court officer needed to hear: "Mr. Paterson, you are an Assistant District Attorney, representing the Queens District Attorney's office and the people of New York State, that guy," and he points to the court officer, "is a doorman and in my opinion if he was a respectable doorman he would get a job at the Ritz or the Plaza or the Waldorf Astoria, rather than being a doorman for robbers, rapists, and killers. Now you get up and go back over there and ask that doorman when he's gonna call our case."

I regained my feet, moved gingerly toward the bench, and asked the court officer the question. He looked like he wanted to jump over the barrier and kill both Annenberg and me but, with hostility, he did tell me what time our case would be up. You would think that seeing me sitting at the prosecutor's table in a three-piece suit, he would not have thought that I was the defendant—but when you're black, that's one of the anomalies of life: on the streets, in department stores, in supermarkets, and now in the courtroom. My salvage from this deflating event was that Annenberg was outraged at what had occurred and knew exactly why it had occurred.

Al Annenberg had very strong right-wing political views, and he didn't work well with women in the office. He loved to have cocktails at lunch and he loved, even more, to have his assistants have cocktails with him, leaving us all to try to enter the courtroom in the afternoon in a hopeless state of inebriation. The rumor in the office was that the district attorney and his advisors liked to match lawyers up with the different bureaus in the office based on their attributes and that they put Al Annenberg in charge of the forensic psychiatric unit because he was, himself, insane. The fact that he wore a dust-mop toupee that even I could see was fake was only a minor issue for him to address. Nonetheless, he became one of my best friends and although I only stayed in the Queens District Attorney's office for two years, he was a cheerleader for me until his death in 1996.

THERE WERE SOME hairy anecdotes attached to the time I worked as an ADA in the Queens office. One time we tried to extend an order of retention for a man named Timothy Tonry. This turned into a horrible tragedy. Tonry had been raised in an orphanage where most of the workers were black. Tonry, as his mental disability developed and intensified, came to hate black people, and one day decided he was going to kill the first two black people he saw. He went to a weapons store and bought one magazine of bullets, it cost $1.24. Tonry had exactly $1.24 in his pocket. What a fatal coincidence that would prove to be. He left the weapons store and killed the first two black people he saw. He was never tried because he was found to be mentally unfit to stand trial and was now being kept in a psychiatric facility. Annenberg came eventually to believe that Tonry's psychiatric condition had improved and that he might be able to stand trial, especially since the crime occurred a long time ago; obviously, this long interval would favor the defense because the evidence and the memories of witnesses were stale, so Annenberg took me to this hearing, which I believe occurred in Orange county, and had me sit to the left of Tonry because, being black, I might antagonize him during questioning. Whether or not this tactic was a factor, it might have worked because Tonry was ordered held in the psychiatric facility for another year.

Then again, the problem was not that, but *this:* Tonry wasn't there that long because he broke out of the facility about two weeks later. I immediately called Annenberg and told him that I wasn't coming to work until they got Tonry back in lockdown because he might be looking for me. I told my boss that the only way I was coming to work was if they sent other assistants to drive me from where I was staying in Hempstead at my parent's house, to Queens, which was a twenty minute drive. Thankfully my fellow ADAs did this for a week and, even more fortunately and thankfully, Tonry was recaptured shortly thereafter.

ON ANOTHER OCCASION, there was a psychiatrist whose name I just don't recall, but the word was that he didn't even talk to his patients: he just wired them up and zapped them with electric shock therapy. This was his solution to every psychiatric problem. Annenberg told us that this doctor's nickname when he first started as a court psychiatrist, and Annenberg was simultaneously just beginning his legal career, was Dr. Electric. Thinking tactically again, Annenberg ordered one of the other ADAs, at a hearing to determine if another defendant was fit to go to trial, to ask this shrink, whatever his name was, if his nickname was Dr. Electric. The ADA refused to do it, so Annenberg went to his go-to guy, who would do anything that Annenberg wanted.

That guy was me.

"Dr. X, are you a licensed psychiatrist in the state of New York?"

"Yes."

"Dr. X, are you a practicing psychiatrist in this state?"

"Yes."

"Dr. X, are you board certified?"

"Yes."

"Dr. X, have you examined defendant Y?"

"Yes."

"Dr. X, have you made a determination based on your medical opinion as to whether this defendant suffers from a mental disease or disability that would impede his capacity to help his attorney?"

"Yes."

"Dr. X, isn't your nickname Dr. Electric?"

The defense attorney catapulted out of his chair and started screaming, the judge banged his gavel and roared at me, "You get out of here, get out of here and don't ever come into my courtroom again."

As I was leaving through the rear door I heard a voice from the middle of the courtroom booming, "That's my guy!"

FINALLY, ON THE last big occasion I recall from those Queens DA years, Al Annenberg got intoxicated at a holiday party. That was no surprise, but as he was leaving the building, he mistook the car of a court officer to be his car. When he went and tried to open the door, miraculously, the door was unlocked and now Annenberg was in the wrong car. The court officer and some of his colleagues see this, and, thinking someone is robbing or stealing the court officer's car, they dragged Annenberg out of the car and beat the crap out of him.

Annenberg didn't come to work the next day and the results of his previous evening's adventures are the major office gossip of the day. Toward the end of the day, the DA himself holds a holiday party—this was the equivalent, for those of us who worked for him, to Moses ascending to the mountaintop to meet the Lord. We actually stood on line to shake his hand. When it was my turn to exchange holiday wishes with John Santucci, the District Attorney of Queens County, I was stunned when the DA addressed me first, "Hey, where were you last night when your boss was at that holiday party?"

I piped up, "Oh, I was home preparing for a case, sir."

And Santucci barked back, "Well, you should have been with your boss last night looking out for him! Why do you think we keep you here?"

In spite of all the memorable times at the Queens DA's office, getting to try cases, getting to conduct hearings in the Supreme Court, and receiving accolades from my colleagues and great friends, such as Annenberg, Mike Cavanagh, Len Livote, and a detective named Judd Bank, the whole time I was inwardly recoiling at the fear of having to take the bar exam. I knew I couldn't pass it. It wasn't that I couldn't learn the material, it's just that the system seemed rigged against me. For one major thing, I couldn't take notes fast enough at the bar review courses. If I taped the courses, then the rehearing of them was taking up too much time. Then again, the books were not readily available on tape because not that many blind people were taking the bar.

But the real problem, which was my fault, was that I'd never decided if I was going to act as a blind or a sighted person in my education, and now my failure to decide that issue was coming back to haunt me. I think what happened, was that at some points there just wasn't a way to handle things, so I just threw out a white flag. But I think that when looking back on it now, I can see why someone in that situation would feel that way. But there weren't many cries for help from me. I didn't think they would be appreciated. I misjudged how things went. So I had a difficult situation due to the things that happened previously, but I didn't raise enough of a concern so that the people that had an inkling, could help me. It's hard for others to come in and ask, and looking back I feel like I've been overly hard on myself for the problems arising from this situation.

Chagrined at this unresolved dilemma and not sharing any of the information with anybody, I resigned from the DA's office in April 1985. Annenberg gave me a going-away party, and people who had worked there fifteen years said they had never had such a good going-away party, but Annenberg really believed in me. In fact, when I came back to the Queens office on a visit a year after leaving, Al was visibly pleased to see me again.

Al Annenberg made my departure a big deal, and I'll always be grateful to him for it.

4

Harlem Shuffles

A s I mentioned earlier, after leaving Annenberg, that's when I went to
work for David Dinkins, who had been the city clerk of New York and
had run for borough president in 1977 and 1981, and who was now running
for borough president in 1985 for a third time and had a very good chance
of winning against an Assemblyman, Jerry Nadler. Nadler would go on to
become a congressman and chair of the Judiciary Committee. I was hired to
be Dinkins's fundraiser. I had been the assistant to his fundraiser in 1981, so
this was a much more comfortable task for me. I took to the job instantly
and performed very well but, inwardly, I was unraveling. I couldn't figure out
how I was going to address this issue with the bar exam. Years later, I would
learn that no blind person passed the bar exam between 1983 and 1988 if I
still remember the numbers correctly. But now there was a group that was
established to try to convince the law examiners that they had to find a
more effective system to create a level playing field for blind candidates and
even for some other differently disabled candidates.

As August began, and the September primary was not far away, I was
feeling anxiety about how much of the staff they'd keep if Dinkins won the
primary—which the polls showed that he would. Certainly, by November, I
would have to figure out what I was going to do. That one question played
over and over again in my mind: *What am I going to do?* I can't go back to
the DA's office, I'm afraid to study for the bar exam, and I was becoming
paralyzed with fear. It's interesting how a minor incident can change the
course of history, especially for one individual, as it did for me that summer
on a night in July—I know it was a Thursday. My best recollection is that it
was July 25, 1985, when David Dinkins was asked to come to a political club
in West Harlem, where the political leader was Alan Hodge.

Dinkins apparently didn't like Alan Hodge too much, and the feeling
was mutual, and I guess this particular evening Dinkins didn't want to go

and allow himself to be berated by the members of Hodge's political organization. Also, Hodge had been previously convicted of stealing cheese from an anti-poverty program and was known as "the cheese thief," which I suspect didn't endear him to Dinkins. The person who usually took Dinkins' place at these events—and I'm not exactly sure who that was—was unavailable, so I was told I should go up and make an appearance. I'd been working on fundraising and really wasn't familiar with borough issues. I sure did think I wouldn't be prepared to handle these issues with only some briefing sheets read to me before the meeting. But I went anyway.

I arrived on time at 7:00 PM to a tense audience. They were not mollified at all that I had come, rather than Dinkins. Mr. Hodge made the introduction and for the next 90 minutes of my life I was bruised, battered, badgered, and beaten by 50 angry people mostly upset that Dinkins wasn't there, but also irate that I didn't understand enough of the issues. Finally, at about 8:30 that evening, the rampage was aborted by Alan Hodge, who advised me that I should not be too upset, that I must understand that Dinkins is running for office, that they are a political club, and that there's no place that David Dinkins should have been that evening other than right there.

In addition, he tells me that the people in that room probably have nothing against me as long as I let Dinkins know how angry they are and how the next time they ask for his audience that they had better get one. I excitedly agreed that I would let Mr. Dinkins know, that I would make him fully aware of all of the political club's concerns. I was about to take a deep breath of relief when a woman sitting approximately in the middle of the crowd, who had raked me over the coals three times already that night, decided that a fourth flogging was in order. She said, "I have one more question." This prompts me to think, *When you're dead, why is it necessary to burn the body? Why do we have to go through this again?* I silently wondered. But I responded, "Absolutely, ma'am, what is your question?"

"First," she said, "I want to tell you that I'm not voting for your candidate because he doesn't have enough respect for those of us who work in the process to come here and let us hear why he thinks he would be a good borough president."

My immediate response was, "That's your decision to make, ma'am."

And she said right over top of me: "But, young man, I have to tell you something; I deeply admire the way you stood here and were gracious and tried to answer our questions, no matter how much we abused you. And what I really want to tell you is; you're a young guy but maybe one day you'll run for office and, when you do, let me know because I'm going to support you."

Shockingly, the audience not only clapped for her but also stood up and clapped for me, giving me a standing ovation. Now my effort was to fight back tears because I was so moved by how the people treated me. They patted me on the back on the way out. This seemed like a minor victory that appeased my conscience because my conscience was still chewing me up over the impending problems with the bar exam. But this ovation would become a major moment about two weeks later when I was in the bedroom of my parents talking to them when my mother took a call from a woman named Bobbi Berlin, who was the chief of staff to our local state senator, Leon Bogues. Unfortunately, she was calling to speak to my father to tell him of the passing of the senator. I knew the senator was ill but I don't think I was expecting that he was not going to survive.

In the Dinkins campaign office the next day, the gossip was already flying about who was going to take his place. And then two days later, I got a phone call at the campaign office from Percy Sutton, a former Manhattan borough president, a former Assemblyman, the head of *Inner City Broadcasting*, and a hero to me. He said that If I was willing to run for that state Senate seat the first $1000 was on him; he also said that he didn't think I would win the race but that this would be a great chance to learn about politics, to learn about other avenues to explore that I might think about as I moved forward. I said, "Mr. Sutton, that is a wonderful offer but the first thing I have to do is pass the bar exam." Mr. Sutton's thoughts on this were straightforward, "Sir, by the time you pass the bar exam, the position will no longer be available." He also suggested that I be very open about my disability; in fact, it may have been one of the first times it was ever said to me in my life. And he ended by telling me that three people who had been in the room when I went to visit Alan Hodge's west Harlem political club were very impressed with my performance, even though they knew that I was unprepared and certainly under attack most of the evening.

This phone call led to a meeting of myself, Bill Lynch, the legendary union organizer in New York who would help nearly a year later to organize the anti-apartheid South Africa parade where I marched with Muhammad Ali and the proverbial Gang of Four—Percy Sutton, Basil Paterson, David Dinkins, and Congressman Charles Rangel.

We talked for about an hour and at the end of it my father said, "This is all very interesting, let's all think this over for about a week and decide which direction we're going to take." Immediately, Sutton turned to my father and said, "Basil, I don't think you understand the purpose of this meeting. We're not discussing the possibility of David running for the Senate—he's running. We came here to get support from the rest of you. Bill Lynch then chimed in his agreement, and Rangel concurred. David Dinkins said he'd support me but he wouldn't mind if I dropped by the office sometime because I was still working for him. Then, my dad, the last hold-out, finally agreed. One thing I always knew about my dad was that you never knew what he was really thinking; after all, this was his son who was running. Yet, in the always brilliant, and mostly out-of-the-box way he thought, he figured why not take the opposite position: make the group bring him around rather than him bringing the group around, after all, it *was* his son.

Nonetheless, I was now a candidate for the state Senate.

EARLIER THAT YEAR, a lifelong friend of mine, Lisa Davis, and I had started a group called The Organization of Concerned New Yorkers. The members were younger, ranging in age from twenty-five to thirty-five, who really wanted to get involved in advocacy on issues, and even in political circles. The group probably had about twenty members and it immediately became my campaign committee. Lisa Davis, whom we used to call "the boss," was basically the spiritual leader of the group. Governor Mario Cuomo designated November 5, the regular Election Day as the special Election Day to fill the seat vacated by the death of Senator Bogues. There was no time to hold a Democratic primary so the county committee for that particular Senate district—in other words, the political leaders on the committee— would choose the Democratic candidate. This candidate would presumably be the next senator because Democrats were winning 90 percent of the votes in this district most of the time.

Originally there were thirteen candidates, and when the first candidates' night was held, I watched the other candidates speak. As I watched and listened I was quietly thinking to myself, *I could beat him, I could also beat him, I could beat her,* and so on down the line. Eventually, I got up and spoke, and then the last few candidates got up to speak. The very last candidate was named Galen Kirkland. I heard him speak and I thought to myself, *OH NO!*

His articulate nature, his warmth toward other people, and his incredible understanding of the issues made him more than a worthy opponent. He had a substantive background in the field of housing, which was a big issue at the time, and this gave him a big advantage. All in all, he was formidable.

As I predicted, the thirteen candidates were quickly whittled down, leaving just Galen Kirkland and me. It just came right down to the two of us. And it really hurt when *The Village Voice* published an article about us called "The Sons of Harlem," written by the late Wayne Barrett. The article appeared two weeks before the election and claimed that I had falsified information on my campaign literature. This allegation quickly became the buzz all over the district. Barrett wrote of me: "He says he was an assistant district attorney even though, in fact, he doesn't have a license to practice law in New York State." I had written in my campaign literature that I had served as an assistant district attorney in spite of not yet being licensed to practice law in New York State. But Barrett buried my full disclosure at the very end of his article, which many people didn't read far enough to learn. Instead, Barrett's article indicated that I had downplayed my lack of a license to practice law: that is, mentioned it only in passing in my campaign literature.

The opposite was true: I had been upfront in my campaign literature about my not having yet passed the bar. Barrett's article, though, if not read to the end, implied that I really hadn't worked as an ADA at all; this implication was doubly ridiculous because I had listed in my campaign literature the people I had worked for and who had paid me as an ADA while I worked there. I hadn't tried to pull a fast one, I hadn't been deceitful, yet I had to deal with this slanted article and overcome it. I was so upset by the gossip the article generated that I actually rolled under my bed just like I was five years old. I thought it would be a safe place, as it sure had been back when I was five.

And then I had an awakening, a moment of clarity. I just decided that; number one, I wished I'd never been a candidate for this position. But then, in a flash, I reversed myself and decided that; number two, now that I was running for this elective office, I couldn't stop running, and I *would just have to win.*

I had appeared at a candidates' night at Joan of Arc High School, located on 97th Street on the West Side of Manhattan, on Tuesday, August 27th. I spent most of my allotted time that night refuting the allegations of

The Village Voice article before the debate turned to questions from the audience. The last question was asked by a gentleman who said that he lived in Harlem and wanted to know if a Harlem resident could ever serve as the state senator for this district. Everybody in the room knew that this state Senate seat, the 29th senatorial district, was what they called a "West Side seat," rather than a "Harlem seat."

In other words, a resident from the West Side always got the nomination and there was no problem because for the past thirty years all of the senators from this district had been black, including judge James Watson, Constance Baker Motley, Reverend H. Carl McCall, who would become the first black comptroller of New York State, and a man named Sidney Von Luther, whose claim to fame was that he once challenged another senator to a duel in the Senate chamber. Leon Bogues, who had just passed away from cancer, freeing up the Senate seat and necessitating the present election, was also black.

Of course, I can't fail to mention that my father, Basil Paterson, had held the seat from 1965–1970, when he ran for lieutenant governor, won the primary, and then ran with former supreme court justice, Arthur Goldberg against Nelson Rockefeller, who had a little bit more money than they did and won the governorship in that election. My father, like several of the preceding black senators, lived in Harlem but was heavily supported by the West Side leaders. But this era preceded a redistricting that subsequently made the Senate seat a given for a resident of the West Side, and this was the state of affairs the man at the meeting had questioned when he asked if the Senate seat was attainable now for a resident of Harlem. There was no great friction or resentment involved. Pretty much, there was an unspoken agreement that this arrangement of a "West Side seat" was how the great Harlem and liberal Upper West Side district worked back then. Yet some people, like the man asking the question, thought it was high time to change this arrangement.

Promptly, as soon as this man raised the last question, all the West Side candidates got up, including Galen Kirkland, and said it didn't matter where you lived, it mattered only what you could offer the district. This was a great statement but totally wrong: residence mattered increasingly to the voters of Harlem, and some wanted the old arrangement, the silent understanding, changed. Now the Harlem candidates got up, and I thought someone was going to shove this fallacy about residence being immaterial right down the throats of its adherents. Surprisingly, this didn't happen. Jim Cappelle,

Miles Matthews, Tony Spencer, Eugene Daniels, and all of the Harlem candidates eschewed the opportunity to challenge this contention that residency and location were a non-issue to win this Senate race.

My confidence had dwindled by now and was certainly not replenished hearing the Harlem candidates agreeing with the West Siders. So, when my turn came to comment—and I was the last speaker—I thought to myself, *This is only a game, I don't play it very well and who cares, this newspaper article has probably killed my chances to win anyway, so I'm just going to get up and say what I feel.* And I did.

"It's very interesting that everybody says that it doesn't matter where you live, but why was the question asked? The question was asked because everybody in this room knows that this is a West Side seat, political leaders on the West Side have been saying it and if somebody doesn't have the guts enough to get up and identify the issue for what it is, then how are they going to go to Albany and represent, with any kind of honesty and character, the real tough issues that people on the West Side and Harlem have?"

Maybe 20 percent of the people clapped, very enthusiastically, but it was still only 20 percent. I sank into my seat in hopeless despair, once again bemoaning the fact that I'd chosen this course in my life. When I returned home I called up my dad and told him what had happened. He said it really didn't sound like it was that bad and I thought that was simply a nice thing for him to say to comfort me, even though I was well aware of what had occurred and the probable consequences. Yet, apparently, my assessment of those probable consequences could not have been more wrong: My decision to stand up and challenge the integrity of the campaign couldn't have been more beneficial.

Late the next afternoon my father called me with boastful enthusiasm to tell me that everyone was telling Congressman Rangel, who had telephoned him an hour earlier, that David Paterson was the only candidate to stand up for Harlem and that the other candidates buckled in fear when a member of the audience challenged the longstanding tradition and party procedure and no one said anything about it except your son. So, Thursday night, two days later, August 29, when I strolled into the Martin Luther King Democratic club in Harlem, which was my home political club, I was feeling no regrets and no recriminations and was all enthusiasm for this latest candidates' night.

On this occasion, the opening statements of all the candidates were very similar. Everybody loved Harlem, some of them grew up in Harlem, some of them worked in Harlem, and so on. Praise for Harlem was on every candidate's lips. They couldn't brag more about how much they loved to represent this district and how great and famous this area was. Once again, I was the last speaker and I took no prisoners.

"Well, well, well, listen to these candidates drowning themselves in joyous harmony. Oh! They love Harlem. They were born in Harlem. They used to work in Harlem. They eat in Harlem restaurants. Their significant other is from Harlem. But you should have heard them two nights ago down on the West Side, they'd never heard of Harlem. They were sanctioning the fraud that this party procedure is being held fairly and that a Harlem resident has a chance to serve the entire district in the New York State Senate. Well I don't care if I win this Senate seat or not at this point but what I do care about is that the leaders and members of this party carry out a procedure in fairness and not in fantasy. And I think that they will. I think once people see that it's time for this process to end—this gentlemen's agreement, this arrangement, this silent covenant or state of affairs; whatever it's been for the past thirty years—it has got to end here and now. I'm going to be your state senator and when I get to Albany and see things that are wrong, I'm going to do something about it. I'm not going to be afraid of any party leaders, any newspapers, or any bosses who think their whims are going to change other people's reality. Harlem has been the epicenter and focus for political activism in this country and the West Side has been a catalyst for change in national policy and they need a state senator that's going to live up to that tradition, that legacy."

It was over: Rangel talked all the Harlem candidates into getting out of the race. Now it was just me against the West Side and with the help of Assemblyman Jerry Nadler, who went on to be congressman Jerry Nadler, I got votes there and won the nomination of the Democratic Party and went on to victory on November 5, 1985. Now I was among the five youngest people ever elected to the New York state Senate. Interestingly, in that campaign, I also got help from two of Jerry Nadler's district leaders, Joyce Miller and Scott Stringer. Incidentally, Stringer is now comptroller with an excellent chance to someday lead New York City.

But the unyielding Galen Kirkland wasn't finished. He and another candidate named Phil Reid, both of whom would become two of my better friends later in life, ran against me in a primary the following year, in 1986. It was a long, hard-fought campaign and it came down to one debate at the Schomburg Library on Malcolm X Boulevard in Harlem. After we covered most of the issues back and forth, it came down to this: each candidate had to give a final statement. These statements would be decisive. Once again I was the last speaker and I decided that I had covered all the issues and was a little tired of the retorts and criticisms from these two other candidates, so I closed my last debate with this summary statement.

"I have listened to Mr. Kirkland and Mr. Reid constantly criticize everything I do. When I come to debates, they want to know why I'm not in Albany, and when I stay in Albany they want to know why I don't come to debates, and there are lots of other types of silly and illegitimate charges."

I paused a moment, then invoked the words of my hero.

"I want all of you in the audience to know that this election will end in the 9th month on the 9th day at 9 o'clock. The polls will close on September 9th at 9 o'clock. 9/9/9. And what I'd like Mr. Reid and Mr. Kirkland to know is you'll be mine when the sign says 9."

This was a prediction that Muhammad Ali had offered to Joe Frasier before their first fight, predicting the round in which Frazier would fall, as Muhammad always did for his boxing opponents. However, my prediction turned out a lot better than his.

But, back to Harlem for a second. Somewhere in the spring of 2000, Exxon Mobil had a proposal to put a pipeline in the Hudson River, running parallel to West Harlem, Washington Heights, Inwood, and starting in the Morningside Heights area of Columbia University. Lacking the political power of other regions around the state, the greater Harlem community was too familiar with what we call "service dumping." All communities have a "not in my back yard" philosophy, but only some can actually implement it. The sewage treatment plant in Harlem that was installed in 1986 was originally scheduled to go in an area in midtown Manhattan, opposite the Penn yards, in 1966. It was pushed up the borough from one community board to the next and the wrangling from influential citizens eventually landed it in Harlem, right next to a marine transfer station very close to a lot of drug rehabilitation centers, homeless shelters, bus depots, and halfway houses.

All the elected officials, district leaders, community board participants, activists, and advocates had a meeting around that time to discuss opposition to the Exxon plan. The salt in the wound after losing the battle over the sewage treatment plant in 1986 was the fact that the plant was treating millions of more gallons of sewage than we were promised, and the survey conducted by one of the agencies found that 24 million gallons of sewage had suddenly disappeared and in their report the plant was compliant even though everybody knew that it was totally fabricated. In addition, incidences of liver cancer in Harlem were reported to be higher since the plant was built.

On one occasion, Governor Mario Cuomo was introducing a new concept called Midnight Basketball, a way to keep people off the streets and in an activity that would be far safer than the trouble they might otherwise find. Just as the governor started to speak, a stiff wind arose, blowing the stench from the treatment plant to the adjacent area where the basketball games would be played. As one of the more vocal agitators about the sewage treatment plant, I was accused of causing the wind to blow in the Governor's direction by his assistant. So that his assistant would feel that he accomplished something that day, I admitted to it. The meeting regarding the Exxon plan was, as it often was in our neighborhood, a contest as to who could find the most creative way to be opposed to it. We addressed the bill of particulars that we had about all these problems to a fare-thee-well. Finally, when the meeting ended we were all asked, "Is there anyone else with a final comment?" I said, "I've decided that I'm actually going to support the Exxon pipeline." You could not believe the surprise and shock that fell over the other participants in the meeting and of course, an explanation was demanded. I said, "What's the worst thing that could happen to the pipeline? Maybe it'll blow up and that'll destroy the sewage treatment plant."

JANUARY 24, 1986. The Empire State Development Corporation, the state agency that assists development in counties all around the state, had a subsidiary, the Harlem Urban Development Corporation—now known as the Harlem Community Development Corporation. All the elected officials served on the board. On this date, they welcomed the two newly-elected officials, Hilton Clark, a councilman who replaced the late Fred Samuels, and myself, who replaced the late Leon Bogues. Clark was a constant antagonist, claiming that the older elected officials didn't share the wealth and opportunity and was constantly castigating everybody because he, for some reason, wasn't a congressman, or a Duke, or whatever he wanted to be.

One of the tasks the board was addressing that day was replacing the chairman of the board. The two choices were Eugene McCabe, the head of North General Hospital, and Eugene Norman, a prominent businessman in his own right. The two Gene's, not only shared the same name but were equal in character, enthusiasm, and work ethic. They were also both close friends of mine so choosing between the two would be difficult. After each made a brief statement, the convener of the meeting wanted to put the issue to a vote. He passed around twenty pieces of paper and asked each member to write which candidate we preferred. Councilman Hilton Clark piped up, "Are these the only candidates we can choose from?"

Donald Cogshill, the executor of the board, said, "No, councilman if there is someone else you'd like to vote for, that is your right. In fact, if you'd like to nominate someone other than the two of them, we'll gladly accept your nomination."

"Oh forget about it," Clarke exclaimed as he grabbed his piece of paper aggressively with hostility and remorse. Straining to pick between my two friends I came up with an alternative idea. Cogshill announced the vote, there were 11 for Eugene Norman, there were 8 votes for Eugene McCabe, and there was one vote for Hilton Clarke. The councilman seemed as bewildered as everyone else in the room for receiving this vote. I didn't vote for myself he offered.

"Sure, you didn't." someone said to him. He became inflamed. "I'm telling you I didn't vote for myself." He responded.

"Methinks the lady doth protest too much" was my offering and that was the end of the meeting. Within a few years, it was also the end of Hilton Clarke, who was beaten in a primary by Virginia Fields, a very competent council member and eventually, borough president. Life went on without Hilton, as it usually did.

MONDAY, JUNE 13, 1994:

I hear that Governor Cuomo, that is Mario, the father, was going to take his basketball team to Lower Manhattan to participate in some events that had begun in San Francisco in 1982. They were held every four years, known as the Gay Games where gay, lesbian, bisexual, transgender, and questioning athletes would participate—sometimes joined by street people—in these competitions. I was pretty athletic as a young person, but never really found a sport in which I could compete, when my father, who was not allowed to take the field when the New York Giants had a tryout in 1949, and hated the Giants ever since, just knew that his son would vindicate his prowess as a baseball player. He also is in the stickball hall of fame. But he found out that it wasn't that his kid couldn't hit the curve, it was that his kid couldn't see the curve, however, he and my brother did understand that athletics were important for a person, even if that person was disabled.

They found, to their surprise, that if they threw a ball at me, I could actually catch it. It was known as a basketball. We mostly played three—hree games in the yard but at times I was actually able to play full court games, particularly if I knew my teammates because they could tell when to throw the ball to me and when not to.

So, I was not particularly pleased when my colleagues from the state Senate would go out and play basketball and not invite me to come. When I invited myself, they thought that was hilarious! So, this is my chance, if Governor Cuomo would let me play on New York's team at the Gay Games, I will be vindicated. The governor welcomed me to play alongside himself and his colleagues, and so on an afternoon later in the week, we took the floor in Greenwich village to play Sweden. The opening tip-off was delayed by the fact that I had a chain around my neck, which was prohibited, and none of the gentlemen who were going to play seemed to be able to get the chain off of me. Whereupon the referee elaborated, "I can't believe we have ten gay men here and we can't get a chain off some guy's neck." As the jewelry was finally separated from my torso, I invited the governor, that if he were to take a rebound and I wave my hand at him, I want him to throw the ball completely down-court. I knew I was the fastest person on the court and figured either I could catch it and lay it up or miss it and it would go out of bounds and that's not such a bad thing. It was that about halfway through the game, Governor Cuomo blocked out a man that had to be six inches taller than him, and retrieved this rebound. I gave him the wave and took off, he threw the ball and, for some reason, I was able to see it in the air and could have caught the ball but I was so nervous that I would drop it that I let it bounce so I could scoop it up and lay it up in the basket, but that gave a pursuer time to catch up to me who ran right into me while I'm trying to shoot the ball as I'm falling. I fling the ball, it hits the backboard, and oh my God, rolls around the rim and in for a basket. The arena went crazy, marveling in my acrobatic shot while I was laying on the floor. Fighting to regain my feet I was confronted by J.J. Gonzalez, a reporter for channel two news in New York. "Senator," he said, "How did you make that shot? Aren't you legally blind?" I looked into the camera and rejoicingly replied, "Well, I guess I got over it." Running down the court, I know that they're going to put this on tv tonight.

With the impending news broadcast, I made sure to notify everyone I knew, family, people I worked with, old friends of mine, people I owed money, and anybody who might be in the vicinity of the WCBS catchment area, so they could watch my athletic triumph at the Gay Games. But the show never came on, I never got to take my victory lap. It just didn't happen.

By the way, would you like to forge a guess about why it didn't happen? Well, here's a clue, remember, it was June 1994, so when we played that basketball game in Greenwich village at the Gay Games, that was the day before the evening that O.J. Simpson drove up the highway in a white Bronco. The NBA championship game between the New York Knicks and the Houston Rockets was preempted. All conscious life in the western hemisphere stopped as the cameras pursued a white Bronco going 5–10 miles an hour up the highway. My former wife had to restrain me as I said, "Kill him, kill the bastard, put the news on!" If I wasn't so upset I might have gone to Channel 2 and got the news footage that they would have used and saved it, but I was too traumatically stressed to think of such a concept that might have mitigated the situation to some degree.

I had to wait five years until 1999 when I competed in the New York City marathon to show off my athletic skill again. Do you know how long a marathon is? Oh twenty-six miles, 385 feet you might surmise, remember that assumes you're standing on the starting line when the race begins. I felt like we were so far in the back that at one point when we were running, in the beginning of the race, I saw all these people on the side and I asked my running partner Patty Ireland, "Who are all those people?"

"That's Mayor Giuliani" she said. "We were at the starting line."

"Well, we've been running for seven or eight minutes and I'm already tired!" But I always appreciated that the Gay and Lesbian community at the Gay games and Governor Cuomo's office gave me a chance to have that magic moment.

JULY 2012:

I left my 4–6 PM radio show on WOR in New York City right on time and arrived in Harlem at about a quarter to seven. I was met by Sali, my barber, who often drove me places, and a gentleman we called inspector Ben, who was a former law enforcement official who worked with Sali, and Tarin Pain. Tarin was a resident in the Lennox Terrace complex in which I lived, and who was recovering from a serious illness and starting to make her way back into the workplace. When I met her on the subway about a month before, I told her that if she'd like to travel with me from time to time, that I would pay her so that I had an assistant to help me negotiate some of the events I attended after my radio show.

On this evening we went to Benta's funeral home in Harlem to attend a wake for a dear friend of mine, Calvin Copeland. Copeland's was a famous restaurant in Harlem on 145th Street between Broadway and Amsterdam Avenue. There was an attempt to expand it to a location on 125th Street, which I believe was known as The Country Kitchen, but the extravagant rent and other competing soul food restaurants in the area made the venture unsuccessful, and I helped Mr. Copeland get assistance from the Empire State Development Corporation to cut his losses. He was a very kind man and beloved in the community, and so I was asked to make a few remarks at the wake. Sali and Ben got us up into the funeral home and Tarin and I walked right up to the front of the reception room where the wake was being held. Appreciative of my attendance, a woman said to me, "You will be the next speaker but as the previous speaker was descending from the stage area a woman came up to me practically in tears and said, "Governor I'm so upset. I don't know how much longer I can stay here. Would you mind terribly if I spoke before you?"

"Absolutely," I replied, "please be my guest." So the woman ascended the stairs and addressed the crowd and I wasn't paying too much attention to what she was saying but I did hear her say that she couldn't sleep the previous Wednesday evening and she couldn't figure out why she couldn't get any sleep and finally she fell off to sleep by 4 o'clock in the morning only to be awakened at 5 o'clock by a phone call to say that her sister had passed away and how difficult this was for her. I'm thinking about what I'm going to say about Mr. Copeland and then suddenly, I wouldn't say a light bulb went off, I'm going to say a light bulb broke, and I turned to Tarin and asked, "Who is in the casket?" And Tarin answered, "A woman." And I retorted, "But we're supposed to be at Calvin Copeland's wake." Tarin contemplated and then offered, "Yeah I've been thinking about that, that's kind of strange."

So, I artfully and cautiously backed into the crowd until I had gotten to the back of the room, which took about three minutes, and exited before the woman finished her remarks. Down the hall, in another room, was Mr. Copeland. They were just ending his ceremony when I walked in and they stopped it and immediately let me get on the stage and it all happened so quickly that I couldn't remember what I wanted to say about Mr. Copeland so I practiced a strategy that I commend to all public speakers. If something is bothering you and you're having trouble getting started, tell the audience how you're feeling or tell the audience what it is that's wrong. So, I recounted the tale to the audience that, had a woman not interrupted me, that I would have given a speech about Mr. Copeland to a room where they were honoring the passing of a member of one of the popular sororities. My admission was met with uproarious laughter and this relaxed me. I went on to talk about the passing of my dear friend. As for Tarin, I just invited her that the next time we went someplace and she had one of these reflective moments, that she might share it with me so I don't embarrass myself in front of the world.

When I got back to the vestibule of the funeral home, I was again greeted by the mourners of Sister Rose. "Thank you so much for coming, Mr. Governor," one of the mourners said to me. "Sister Rose was such a special person. I just felt I had to be here," I replied.

5

Now, About This Slavery

When Columbus sailed the ocean blue in 1492, it has been believed that two members of his party were of African descent. When Balboa discovered the Pacific Ocean, it is estimated there were thirty Blacks in his party. So, the first Africans to come to the United States did not come as slaves but rather as explorers. One, known as Esteban—or Estebanico—was quite prolific in his success, mapping out a large part of the new region. Settlers from Europe reached Jamestown in 1607 and established a slave market by 1619.

It should be remembered that Blacks were not the first group enslaved in the new world. The settlers attempted to bond the Indians who had embraced the European immigrants when they arrived at Plymouth Rock and other locations. The Native people totally resisted this siege. They were aware that this was their land. They observed their traditions and upheld their principles. When forced into bondage against their will, they exercised a value that would be echoed years later by one of the American Revolutionary heroes, Patrick Henry who exclaimed "Give Me Liberty or Give Me Death."

This is way the settlers separated the enslaved Africans from their families, discouraged any education and lynched many for the slightest infraction. Speaking of the practice, a plantation owner named Willie Lynch wrote an entire thesis on the method of destroying any self-awareness among the enslaved Africans.

Meanwhile, the Indians were driven from their land and ravished nearly into extinction. In 1972, the Nixon administration re-identified the so called "Indians" to be referred to as Native Americans. Later in the decade, Russell Means, one of the leaders of a famous uprising in Wounded Knee South Dakota, would remark that "Indian means 'the People of God.'" I would rather be known in this fashion rather than branded with a title by the United States Government.

Interestingly enough, the importation of slaves by 1800 had been banned in every state, with the exception of the state of Georgia. But the smuggling of slaves was big business and there were slaves present in every state, including New York. Finally, in 1799 New York passed an emancipation law that banned slavery; this being twelve years after the adoption of the United States Constitution. No other document, including the Magna Carta, should be heralded as much as the American Constitution which was a true attempt to create freedoms for the most number of people, but the original Constitution did nothing for the slaves, and the residue of that hypocrisy has been a crucible for the United States that has lasted up until today.

It's safe to say that although living standards have risen since the adoption of the Constitution, for many, their standard of living has stayed the same. The number of slaves in New York, about twenty thousand in 1787 when the Constitution was passed, is about the same amount of homeless people who wander the streets of our city today. The good news is that Reverend Dr. Martin Luther King Jr.'s *Arc of Freedom* is bending toward justice, and anyone who doesn't think there has been a mammoth improvement in race relations in this country bends towards delusion, but anyone who thinks we are living in a post-racial period, is a charlatan.

The original Constitution gave slaves nothing, article one, section two, clause three; providing how to count the population in order to determine the appointment of taxes and of congressmen, counted slaves as 3/5ths of their actual number. In other words, according to Judge James Watson—a predecessor of mine in the state Senate, now deceased—if there were 200 Blacks on a plantation, they would be counted as 120 people. We would be remiss to forget to say that the slaveholders cast the votes for their slaves, thereby turning their fractional personhood into a means of further enslavement. The fact that two Blacks out of five counted for nothing may be the formal beginning of the black as the invisible person in American history, but it counted for the state of Virginia, which had one quarter of the electoral votes of the state of Pennsylvania, but with this "three fifths of a man" doctrine, the two states had equal representation when electing a president. The Constitution also included article four, section two, clause three, which had a special provision for runaway slaves providing that they could not become free by escaping into another state but *shall be delivered upon-claim of the party to whom such service or labor may be due.*" This clause is still in the Constitution today, although the edition in which I read it, explains in a cautious, lawyerly way, that it *"appears obsolete in view of the provisions of amendment thirteen prohibiting slavery."* I certainly hope no one in the Trump administration finds this section.

Oddly enough, the original Constitution considered slavery to be a matter under the control of the states. It might also interest you to know that Thomas Jefferson, who would later become our third President, struggled with the race issue personally and professionally. His first draft of the Declaration of Independence used Judge James Watson's description of the slave trade as *"cruel war against human nature itself, violating its most sacred rights of life and liberty."* Unfortunately, those lines did not make the final cut after they were opposed by a coalition of New England Slave traders and southern planters.

President Jefferson's true feelings survived his death in 1826 when he manumitted that all of his slaves would be freed. In an odd quirk of history, he gave those slaves independence upon his death on July 4, 1826, the fiftieth anniversary of Independence Day and also the day that the second president of the United States, John Adams, passed away.

In the first half of the nineteenth-century, slavery became entrenched in the south due to the tremendous success of cotton cultivation and the invention of the cotton gin by Eli Whitney, a machine that effectively separated the cotton fiber from the seeds, husks, and foreign material. It may be that the main reason why slavery really did not thrive in the north was that the economy of the northern states did not manage to develop any major business enterprises in which the exploitation of Blacks was exceptionally profitable. In any event, in an environment in which the economic incentive for promoting slavery was not paramount, a spirit of natural revulsion for slavery began to flourish and the abolition of slavery became a political force. But the abolition of slavery had no foundation in the Constitution— its moral strength derived from the more basic concepts of justice and liberty that Jefferson had drafted in the original draft of the Declaration of Independence.

Between 1800 and 1860, the big question was always what to do about slavery when new territories and states were being added to the United States. For instance, the Louisiana territory, acquired in 1803, was divided according to the Missouri compromise of 1820, in which the state of Missouri was admitted with slavery, but slavery was excluded in territories north of the 36th parallel. Parallels, of course, being the horizontal lines that divide the earth's circumference. President Jefferson, five years before his death, divided the circumference some more by saying, "in the gloomiest moment of the revolutionary war, I never had any apprehension equal to what I feel from this source." In the same year, the great English minister and wit, Sidney Smith, writing in the *Edinburgh Review*, asked mockingly, "Under which of the old tyrannical governments of Europe is every sixth man a slave, whom his fellow creatures may buy, sell and torture?" Texas thereafter entered the Union as a slave state. Later, the compromise of 1850, brought in California as a free state, left Utah and New Mexico as neutral territories, abolished slavery in the District of Columbia, and passed the Fugitive Slave Act to disrupt the Underground Railroad. Then all hell broke loose in a dispute over Kansas and Nebraska in 1854, in the course of which, the Missouri Compromise was repealed, and on the books, slavery was no longer barred in the northern part of the Louisiana Purchase.

This led to an 1857 decision by the United States Supreme Court that held, among other things, that Congress had no power, under the Constitution, to enact the Missouri compromise, meaning that it had no power to restrict slavery within the United States. This was the famous Dred Scott decision in which Mr. Scott claimed that, by virtue of his having resided, with the consent of his master, in Illinois—a territory in which slavery was forbidden—he had become free. The opinion of Chief Justice Taney also stated that Scott was not a citizen within the meaning of the Constitution, and did not have the right to sue in federal court. The multiple edicts in this supreme court case in which the court held 7-to-2, had to be the darkest day in the abolitionist movement to try to free the slaves. It summarily held that Dred Scott, by virtue of his being black, could not be considered five fifths of a human being, and therefore could not sue in court. It was the darkest day, but in light of events that occur these days, and events that can occur in one's own life, it sends an important message.

Looking back on history and that slow curve of Dr. King's Arc of Justice, isn't it interesting to note—as a Brooklyn minister named Herbert Daughtry once pointed out at a Martin Luther King Jr. memorial celebration—that the decision in the great Dred Scott case actually occurred within six years of President Abraham Lincoln's signing of the Emancipation Proclamation on January 1, 1863. In fact, Since Lincoln issued the Emancipation Proclamation as a military measure, it didn't apply to border slave states like Delaware, Maryland, Kentucky, and Missouri, all of which had remained loyal to the Union. For this reason, it had to be amended, and that signing occurring on Sept 22, 1863. Nonetheless, Reverend Daughtry's message was that no matter how dark the hour, no matter how painful the struggle, no matter how bleak may be the opportunities, if you keep working to achieve justice, you might be just around the corner from freedom. So, after a bloody civil war and the thirteenth amendment to the Constitution in 1865, festering moral cancer of slavery finally ended.

A very interesting sidelight of research was the discovery that, in certain circumstances, the status of Blacks as property had an ironic advantage. Thus in 1861 when three fugitive slaves sought refuge in a union military camp at Fort Monroe, Virginia, one of the grounds given by General Benjamin F. Butler in refusing to return them, was that in as much as they were fit to work in the trenches, they were property, liable to be used in aid of the rebellion and therefore he claimed them as contraband of war. For many years after, contraband, as a slang term for Blacks or slaves, was widely used. One wonders what might have happened if the term had not gone out of use. It's possible, that in the twentieth century, especially in the Reagan administration, that the term contraband would have been shortened to contras, and who knows what special benefits may have flowed to these Blacks.

So, slavery basically still existed even after the Emancipation Proclamation. The slaves became sharecroppers and were mistreated almost as badly as they had been when in chains. There were an estimated eight thousand lynchings in the south between the end of the civil war and the Brown vs The Board of Education decision in 1954. The simple fact is that only in the last generation, have men and women of African descent and other minorities, begun to participate in a noticeable way in the experience of power, resulting with the election of Barack Obama in 2008. The reality is that we have broken the chains of servitude but, to some, the mental image of its degradation still arises whenever they look at black people and, to many black people, the illusion that the chains still exist is an impediment to any progress.

In 2010, I wrote a letter as Governor to the Secretary of the Interior to support the Federal Government's Recognition of the Shinnecock Indians of Eastern Long Island as an official Nation. This movement for instatement began a half century earlier, but met with success that year. The Shinnecock honored me in 2011 in South Hampton for my efforts; one of the happiest moments of my life.

In 2007 when I was Lt. Governor, I accompanied the American Jewish Committee to Israel for a conference on alternative energy. A well-known conflict in the middle east for over five thousand years, impinged itself on the activity of the gathering and we had some speakers from the Israeli government and even a Palestinian professor, who addressed the group artfully. My chief of staff, Charles O'Byrne and I contacted the professor and had lunch with him the next day in Jerusalem. Over lunch, I asked him about a couple of violations that the UN had placed on Israel for some attacks over the years and asked him why it happened. Quite predictably, he said; "Because they are sick." Then I asked him about September 11 and various other terrorist attacks and consistent threats to blow Israel off the map. "Why did that happen?" He thought for a moment and said to me, "Because we are sick."

My dear reader, the lugubrious effect of slavery on our livelihoods over 150 years after its legal termination, still plagues this country. Whenever there is a major domination of one group of people over another, that includes brutality, separating babies from their mothers, raping their mothers, killing people indiscriminately, and taking their names and languages away from them, you're going to have this result. We don't even have to go back a hundred years to witness the savage slaughter of 6 million Jews at the hands of Nazi Germany and its conquered territories, but the valued resurgence of the descendants of this horrible demonstration of evil offers hope. Each of us comes onto this planet unarmed, our brain is our only weapon and we've demonstrated technological advances far beyond the comprehension or imagination of our ancestors. However, the same hateful and uncivilized notions continue to dictate and pervade almost all of our histories. At times, to many who've suffered due to this oppression—and for those who have tried for years to undo it—it must seem unending, but giving up on mankind's quest for humanity is not an option. In the end, it's really quite simple. It could be summed up in five words. We are all the same. We all came from the same place. If we believe in a higher power, as I do, if we are atheists, if we believe in a multiverse, whatever we believe, all research and documentation of history, points toward the fact that we have grown out of an original group that literally went forth and multiplied.

Here is where Darwin and Adam & Eve could agree. *Therefore, those individuals who revel in tirades against those who they believe are taking things away from them, and others who believe they have been systemically denied*

opportunities for their whole lives will never achieve until they look into the eyes
of each other and realize that they are brothers and sisters.

So, the seeds of humanity and discord are planted in all of us and each
must become—before life has flown—a stumbling block or a stepping stone:

> **Princes & Kings**
> *Isn't it strange how princes and kings,*
> *and clowns that caper in sawdust rings,*
> *and common people, like you and me,*
> *are builders for eternity?*
>
> *Each is given a list of rules;*
> *a shapeless mass; a bag of tools.*
> *And each must fashion, ere life is flown,*
> *A stumbling block, or a Stepping-Stone.*
> —R. Lee Sharpe

NONE OF US seem particularly willing to accept this reality but it is reflected
in most philosophical and spiritual works, my favorite of which is the book;
The Spontaneous Fulfilment of Desire by Deepak Chopra. He submits to the
belief that none of us would ever compare ourselves to Hitler, but then simply asks, which one of us is without prejudice, the extent of prejudice is not
confined by the lines of race, religion, national origin, or sexual preference.
It can be ignited by age, disability, physical appearance, political affiliation
and judgmental presumptions made against individuals with whom someone has first met, based on the slightest data. How many times have you
heard someone say, "I didn't like her from the first minute I met her?" This
invites a belief that instinctive reactions to others are infallible, when in
fact, they are most often generated by fear, so the judgments promulgated by
our instant notice of someone else's difference based on their accent, color
of their skin, or choice of footwear, is not based on the infallibility of our
own psychic energy but rather is described by Deepak Chopra as the ego
having a conversation with itself. Being black and blind, I never thought I
would be in charge of anything because half the time I couldn't figure out
which disability was hindering my progress. Eventually, I learned that bifur-
cating my struggles was not the way to solve my problems. When I looked
at life holistically, I realized that I have been blessed with a unique vantage
point in life.

When I was seventeen, it wasn't a very good year. I was discriminated against by fellow blind students who were participating in a precollege training program in Syracuse, New York. Two years later I was turned down for employment by a family friend whose wife had been a special education teacher and advocate for me—and he himself, a leader in the local NAACP, because of my blindness. Twenty years later it was a much better time when I read the book, *The Power of Myth* by Joseph Campbell and William Moyers. Campbell posits that mankind is too often confined in what he calls a bonded field, which is, that I only like people who wear my costume or live near my house. But in the end, charity begins at home. We would all be better off spending a lot more time ameliorating some of our own imperfections and trying, at least, to treat people the way we tell people that we do.

In the summer of 1978, I finished my first year of law school at Hofstra University. At age 24 I was hired for summer employment as a summer associate in the firm Stroock & Stroock & Levan, by my longtime dear friend Chuck Moerdler and his son Geoff. There was a deposition involving an explosion at a Texas oil refinery when someone suggested, to speed things up, we order lunch in. Many of the lawyers involved on both sides of this case were Jewish and during the lunch discussion, one attorney recounted the fact that he had worked for the law firm Sherman and Sterling, one of the major firms at the time, for ten years. He excelled in his performance but was not offered a partnership at that firm. It seemed that eight other voices chimed in within moments, discussing their discrimination as Jews in the legal profession. In my naïve state of confusion at the time, I didn't think Jews had any problems. Growing up in Hempstead New York with a lot of Jewish friends, I thought they all excelled and their families were doing great. But as I listened to these elocutions of hardship and unfair treatment, I thought to myself, *I could close my eyes, change a couple of accents and I would be sitting where I was most comfortable, with a bunch of black lawyers, complaining about opportunities that slipped through their hands, state contracts that never came their way, clients who would be interested until they came to the office and saw who they were and then sought other legal counsel.*

At that point, I had an epiphany. The reason I was not as sympathetic or better-informed about the travails of another disenfranchised group, was because I had oversaturated myself with negativity, based on real, but at the same time, overemphasized examples of unfair treatment. I resented what I perceived as black people being black, but white people not even really being white. They were just people. Nobody pulled their cars over, like many police did, and insulted them even when they didn't do anything wrong. Nobody followed them around department stores. No one asked them in conversation about what it was like to be white and no one chastised them for complaining about conditions that everyone knew were unequal.

Around that time, I went to see some friends of mine who worked for a very popular FM radio station. It was an R 'n' B station that employed mostly blacks but some whites, and I found that the whites had suddenly symbolically become black. They were ridiculed for not understanding the culture and reviled for demonstrating the slightest naivete. Now there are some white people who think that this exchange of bigotry is even. They've become outraged at having to take a sip of what black people have had to gulp in gallons for the last couple of centuries. There were a hundred other radio stations where I saw what was happening in reverse but the point is; that degradation that makes us feel inferior is one of the lethal problems we have not solved in our society.

One of the civil rights activists from the 1960s, Stokley Carmichael, used to say that blackness isn't as much a color as it is a condition. There were poor whites that lived in the south whose circumstances weren't that much greater than the Blacks, but the government made them feel far superior because of the discrimination in public accommodations and educational opportunity. The only happiness they ever derived was from the fact that there were those who were lower on the totem pole than they were. In terms of real, concrete material benefits, they were also black because the overall society denied them the opportunity to get out of their poverty and lead productive lives. Young people orphaned by their parents, victims of child sexual abuse, veterans returning from Vietnam, and the elderly were all victimized in analogous ways to the subjugation of black Americans. You never know when experience creates knowledge right at your doorstep. That epiphany in the conference room at Stroock & Stroock & Levan enlightened my values for public service, which I would begin seven years later.

As a state senator representing Harlem and the Upper West Side in the late 1980s—two communities with similar ideological points of view but varying cultural patterns and a profound misunderstanding of each other's plight—gave me opportunities that I remember to this day. I noticed that a number of not-for-profits specializing in landmark preservation were working on the west side to preserve cultural and artistic sites that were being demolished in favor of huge apartment buildings and eateries. Around that time a well-known night-life haven in Harlem known as *The Baby Grand* was closed to make room for a commercial appliance store. I brought the westside landmark experts to Harlem where they taught us how to use New York City's landmarks preservation commission to stop these attacks on the rich history and culture of one of the world's most famous neighborhoods. Similarly, a resident of 92nd Street and Broadway, who recognized that drug dealing was now rampant in that particular area, went out and threatened the drug dealers with police action. Unfortunately, in the ensuing weeks, this woman was murdered. This was a horrible consequence for brave leadership by a concerned citizen.

I took block association leaders from Harlem, who were aware of these similar circumstances but had become familiar about ways to contact the police department without giving any indication to drug dealers that this was going on. In each of the cases, I used the strengths of the other community's experience to educate the most recent victims of difficult circumstances.

Some say that the universe is more than 14 billion years old and its dimensions are immeasurable, but its vastness confuses us about the simplicity of life.

In the end, the universe is within us.

6

The Forgotten History

Just incidentally, amid 244 years of slavery and ninety-two additional years of legalized segregation, there is yet another abhorrence that many black people and even many white people feel about American government and its subsidiaries up until this very day. It is a deep-seated contempt perhaps even a hatred for the contributions and even the sacrifices that blacks have made to make America great. We've heard these stories before. The segregation of black soldiers from whites during the first and second World Wars, even when they were allegedly fighting for the freedom of the same country. The theft of artistry and performance of black musicians, only to be rebranded for a white audience with credit given to other authors, and the failure to recognize excellence in the fields of medicine, science, law, literature, education, and art, as well as contributions to military and public service.

In 2019, a *New York Times* reporter offered a series of articles and blogs entitled "The 1619 Project." It documented the four hundredth anniversary of the establishment of slavery by the settlers. It chronicles the struggle for freedom for the slaves and how its success vindicated the promises of the Declaration of Independence and our founding Constitution. These historical revelations were lampooned by a number of news outlets and blogs who scolded the author, Nicole Hannah Jones, that she would do better to focus her attention on the greatest achievements of American history.

Perhaps this gives context to a recent *CBS News this Morning* report that exposes the treatment of slavery and the Civil War in current grade school history books. The children in some states are reading that the Civil War was a fight between the North and the South over states' rights, and not mentioning slavery at all. Counties in the state of Texas teach their children that the Blacks from Africa were selected to come to Texas to help with chores on the plantations. Without the research of Mrs. Jones, CBS, and others who set the record straight, the bogus history that is still spewing from antagonistic forces would be accepted as reality.

But of all the suffered indignities there are none that probably matches this still relatively unknown fact whose discovery will offend whites as well as Blacks, Hispanics, and Asians. I call it the forgotten Memorial Day, whose secret would have remained unknown had it not been brought to our attention by lauded professor of history at Yale University, David Blight.

As director of the Gilbert Lehrman Center for the Study of Slavery at Yale, Blight's article, printed Memorial Day of 2011, proposed that black people invented Memorial Day. The history revealed is that, even after the surrender of the Confederates that ended the Civil War, hundreds of African-American soldiers—most of them from the 21st Infantry—were held captive at an old racetrack in South Carolina. Due to horrendous living conditions including malnutrition and violence, 257 of these men died and were buried in a mass grave. This barbaric tragedy took place in South Carolina where black workers came together to resurrect their remains and bury them in individual tombs. According to Professor Blight, who found this historic information archives at Harvard University, a celebration of the soldiers was held on Monday, May 1, 1865. It was called the Tribute to the Heroes of the Cemetery, but some called it the first Decoration Day because of the roses carried by children in this epic parade alongside their mothers who were adorned with baskets of flowers as they marched with the black infantrymen and the workers of the town who awarded the proper burial for these brave black soldiers. Nearly ten thousand freed Blacks marched in this occasion where they squeezed into the race track and jockey club to hear the messages of four black preachers, listened to spirituals such as "John Brown's Body," and concluded by singing "The Star-Spangled Banner." This was the largest of many Memorial Day events that were held throughout the South. The African-American origins of the holiday were later suppressed according to Dr. Blight, by white southerners who reclaimed power as their states gained readmission to the union and reconstruction came to an end. The holiday was then reinterpreted to mark the sacrifices of white Americans who fought on both sides of the war in a gesture of reconciliation.

Dr. Blight wrote "In the memory of the events of history, some stories get remembered and some get cast aside." Clearly the Southern narrative of Memorial Day became accepted nationally in what Frederick Douglass proclaimed as a "false equivalency" when he spoke on Memorial Day at

Arlington National Cemetery in 1871. Douglass eviscerated the notion that the celebration of Memorial Day is a celebration of two different cultures fighting for what they each thought was right. Douglass made it clear that the South violated all standards of human rights and tried to destroy the rest of the country's movement toward righting the wrongs of history. Nonetheless, the horror of this carnage which occurred within days of the assassination of President Lincoln, ignited the spirit of the newly-freed Blacks who took their meager supplies and performed the most honorable of ceremonies for those who gave their lives for freedom. It should come as no surprise that different websites and other historians dispute the renderings of Professor Blight's research.

My question is, why did history accept the South's version of the holiday's origin? According to Professor Blight, the date of May 30, 1868, was set as what we previously recognized as the first Memorial Day. On that date, a ceremony was held at Arlington National Cemetery in Washington, DC. Once again, a display of enriched history was either challenged for its authenticity or admonished for staining the wonderful contributions of the American settlers.

I dedicate this chapter to my late uncle, Otis Hairston, who fought in Germany during World War II. When I was thirteen, he explained to me that the white soldiers showed more respect and kindness toward the German prisoners of war than their fellow troops. On one occasion, the POWs were allowed to sit in a van while the black soldiers were ordered to clear a path through a wooded area. When the dismayed soldiers confronted their white counterparts, one of them remarked that, "When I follow you guys up a hill shooting at the Germans, I really don't know the difference between them and you." This was certainly a dangerous threat, so much so that the policy was reversed.

Most Americans, when queried, denied any relationship to the acts of their ancestors in the past. However, they freely invoke the editorial "we" when marveling over the way the new world was settled with victories in the Revolutionary War and the War of 1812. Even the emancipation of the slaves is counted among the greatest hits of American triumph. As to why this barbaric system was imposed in the first place we can only ponder, but it seems that amnesia, rather than a demonstration of contrition, has been the response—much like what Germany attempted to do, post-Holocaust. We have buried our heads, as did Japan, when they attacked China and the US eighty years ago.

Here-here to the unknown black soldiers. Here-here to the newly freed black residents of Charleston, South Carolina, who honored the Martyrs of the Race Course, in 1865. But that is not all; bravo to the men and women of all colors who have fought for our nation. Let not the wrongs of the past obfuscate our commitment to each other, with reckless leadership and partisan disinformation infecting the airwaves. In the time of corona, I propose that we hold a march to commemorate this forgotten history of heroism that occurred over 150 years ago.

Recently, the Minneapolis killing of George Floyd has evoked a multiplicity of anger similar to that of the black soldier toward his fellow troops in Germany. Initially the frequent law enforcement response by turning information into disinformation was applied. But, when a seventeen-year-old bystander released the now damning video of the incident to the media, the "One bad apple" doctrine was invoked in response. Nowhere did anyone want to assign responsibility for this obvious malfeasance of justice. Amidst the rage that many of us feel as we count Mr. Floyd among other victims of police misconduct—such as Eric Garner, Amadou Diallo and Breonna Taylor—there are solid and substantial truisms that we must confront to ameliorate so much injustice.

The primary of which is that the police and law enforcement as a whole are beloved by the American public. To most citizens, police officers are not just their protectors; they are their neighbors, as well. They are the guys using the lane next to yours at the bowling alley. They are little league coaches, scout leaders, and deacons at the church. At the same time they work long hours, often underpaid, and are always risking their lives. They rightly inherit the reputations of their predecessors only in cases of corruption does the public feel betrayed by the cops. As long as officers are on duty, they enjoy the benefits of all doubt.

The reality is that too many law enforcement personnel do not live in the communities that they serve, have little experience with those who don't look like them, and buy into byzantine stereotypes pertaining to minorities and particularly black men. Jenna Moldaver, a young student writing in a Vanderbilt University newspaper, admonished her white student colleagues that her syllabus, where she attended high school in New Jersey, did not include one writing of an African American author. It isn't just the police whose education caused them to look at the world through an obfuscated prism, but in law enforcement the result of this cultural disparity has produced eye opening comparisons between the frequencies when force is utilized to apprehend a black man as opposed to a white man. In addition, a staggering statistic informs us that when prosecutors sought the death penalty in criminal cases in the last quarter of the 20th Century that it was applied twice as often when the defendant was black.

When beleaguered community leaders try to raise these issues in pursuit of equal treatment they were confronted by insults that labeled their pleas as outrageous, illegitimate and un-American.

Another obstacle to justice for victims of police brutality has been those who resort to violence themselves in response. In doing so they have often damaged property and destroyed businesses in their own neighborhood. Displays of arson, looting and attacks on the police must be condemned out of hand. Many have blamed left wing operatives for stirring up the otherwise peaceful protesters. They might have a point, but they should be reminded that those of their ilk who have been traditionally and antagonistic to the progress of black people made these same allegations in reaction to the riots in the '60s. Investigations exposed that the FBI's COINTELPRO, short for counterintelligence program, exhorted riots at the behest of its director J. Edgar Hoover.

Gill Nobel hosted a weekly ABC interview program, until his death in 2012. In 1980, he interviewed a former FBI undercover agent named Darthard Perry. In addition to posing as a black revolutionary, Mr. Perry confessed to burning down a prominent performing arts theater and then blaming it on white subversives. This was a catalyst for the Watts riot in 1967. Hoover's intent was to destabilize the civil rights movement, which he claimed was a threat to national security.

But if there is a silver lining around this dark cloud of repeated injustice, with little redress, it may be the surprising and uplifting intervention of whites, Asians, and Hispanics in this process. Overwhelming crowds of protectors have filled the streets in all 50 States and many international cities. Entertainers and athletes known to live in a bubble of self-indulgence have been demonstrating, contributing and taking personal risk to fight for justice in this case. Even members of law enforcement, including high ranking officials have displayed the leadership in this period that may become the foundation of efforts to bring a higher level of professionalism that the criminal justice system sorely needs. These are welcome and unprecedented actions that bring hope for the future, and yet there still remains a provincial attitude that thwarts all efforts for change. I call it the new racism. It denies the existence of racism itself and takes no responsibility for inequality. It relates sincere efforts for diversity to anarchy, communism, terrorism or any label deemed to frighten the public. But even as we cut through this schizophrenic veil of elitist sophistry, we are constantly confronted with real obstacles and phony remedies.

We've always been dazzled by the oration of Dr. King, but in this current turmoil I suggest we employ his methods which are equally amazing. It should be noted that Dr. King only chose to publicize examples of injustice that would enlighten observers to the terrible conditions under which millions of blacks lived at that time. He thought that the opportunity for change was so precious that it could not give way to any distractions. For example, other blacks had been arrested for failure to sit in the back of buses prior to the legendary action of Rosa Parks in 1955. King did not wish to stage an incident; he waited for the right moment. Because of the abject hatred of black men in the south at that time, King believed that public sentiment would favor a woman victim of such an egregious policy. An arrest was made when a black woman refused to sit in the back of a bus, soon after but in the process she punched a police officer in the jaw. King declined to act. Then another woman was taken into custody for the same offense; in her case it was learned that she had a baby out of wedlock. There is nothing wrong with being an unwed mother, but in the 1950's south, King determined that the condemnation of this woman by religious leaders and the criticism of leadership for supporting her would drown out the principal of civil rights. Rosa Parks had a history of community involvement and social activism. When she refused to comply with the southern tradition, she was well equipped to handle the mission and the rest is history. So let's learn from history. Shrill cries to defund police departments and other retaliation will not resolve this issue. What we need is a whole new concept of policing and retraining of officers. That will take more funding, but as Dr. King said "You can tell where a nation's heart is by how it spends its money."

In the coming months detractors will attempt to sully the reputation of George Floyd they will impugn his character and publicize every mistake he ever made. But they will never erase the image of a man strangled on the ground at the hands of a police officer. The number 8,46, which tabulates the minutes and seconds that officer applied a knee to his neck, strikingly coincide with the number 8:46, which denotes the time of day that the first plane hit the World Trade Center in 2001. I believe that to be the worst tragedy in American history. In the present case, the premature death of George Floyd is one of many incidents, seen or not seen, which chronicle the worst history of Americans. Let's remember that every American, regardless of the charge, is allowed their date in court. Sometime next year this officer will receive his fair trial. And I know the perfect day on which it should be held; the day marking one year from the date of Mr. Floyd's death; a date known as Memorial Day.

7

The Real Skeletons in the Closet

January 3, 1986:

I was in the New York State Senate and, strangely, I had already been in the New York State Senate on December 8, 1985. We had a special session to deal with a health care issue. I don't think I understood what we were doing, I just did what the other members of the Senate minority told me to do but it all seemed like an illusion now. This was the first day of legislative session for the year, and the Senate and assembly would meet in joint session to hear the governor's State of the State Address. Each house of the legislature had to send two representatives to the governor's office to notify him that the legislature was awaiting his address. When possible, the leaders of the legislature would send the newest member to deliver this information. The Republicans held the majority in the New York State Senate and there were no new members from their side that joined the chamber, so they sent a very fine gentleman, Syracuse senator John De Francisco. I was sent from the Senate minority to represent us in this meeting with the governor. In the brief and obligatory meeting, both senator De Francisco and Governor Mario Cuomo welcomed me to the Senate. At some point in the meeting, Governor Cuomo talked about the hall of fame pitcher Sandy Koufax. When I recounted to the governor how Koufax had come back after only two days' rest to pitch the seventh game of the world series in 1965, allowing the Dodgers to escape and win the series from the Minnesota twins, Governor Cuomo looked at Senator De Francisco and said, "I didn't think he was old enough to remember any of that."

As I walked onto the Senate floor with my chief of staff Geoffrey Garfield, Geoffrey pointed out to me that one of the candidates who ran against me, the Republican candidate in the 1985 special election, Joe Holland, was in the chamber standing on the Republican side of the aisle.

Garfield remarked, "He only received 12 percent of the vote, doesn't he know he lost, or he is here to challenge your validity to take the seat!" So, I went over to Joe and said;

"How you doing?"

"Fine!"

"How were the holidays?"

"Great!"

All along I'm trying to move him to why he's standing in the chamber when I won the election. So finally, I discontinued the manipulative retorts and just said, "So what brings you to Albany, Joe?" Holland turns to me and says, "I want to introduce you to senator John Daly, he represents the region that encompasses Niagara Falls, he's also the chair of the Senate housing committee."

"Pleased to meet you." I offered to Senator Daly,

"Welcome senator Paterson, I worked with your father years ago and I am so happy that a member of your community is going to be counsel to the Senate housing committee."

Astonished, and a little embarrassed, I maintained my composure and shook hands with other members of the Senate that they introduced me to and then walked back to my seat in the chamber, where Garfield informed me that the counsel for the housing committee probably makes 50 percent more than you do, so it's really not clear who came out the best in this election. Joe Holland would actually go on to become a commissioner years later in the Pataki administration. He was a true renaissance man, as he owned a restaurant, a beauty aids store, developed housing, was a strong supporter of the arts, and always an impactful figure any place he went. Most recently he took a flyer on a gubernatorial candidacy in 2018.

As for me, the freshman year in the Senate was far less eventful than my first foray into the chamber. I'd staved off two opponents in the primary and won a convincing margin in the general election. I went to a nighttime Christmas party on Friday, December 19, on the held by my dear friends Paul and Amy Williams on the Upper West Side. Relaxing the next morning and preparing for holiday shopping, I heard a story on the radio about some kind of an attack that left a man dead after he ran onto the Belt Parkway in Queens to avoid his pursuers. Forever this will be known as the Howard Beach case, as it commenced in that venue. Four African-American men driving through the area experienced car trouble, one man remained to look after the car, 3 others went to seek assistance. As they were exiting a local pizza parlor, somewhere between eight and twelve white troublemakers from the area confronted them. They were chased through the streets. One member of the party, the late Cedric Sanderford, was injured in the melee. Michael Griffiths, who was his girlfriend's son, was chased onto the Belt Parkway where he was accidentally run over by a driver who couldn't stop his car. The families of the victims complained that law enforcement spent more time investigating them than apprehending the perpetrators.

About a week and a half later, Bill Lynch, now chief-of-staff to Borough President David Dinkins, invited me to a meeting to demand justice for the victims of this bias-related violence. I say bias-related because, the mob chasing the individuals were white and they, were black. Other than the borough president, the only other elected official in the room was my dear friend, Assemblyman Roger Green, then the chair of the black and Puerto Rican legislative caucus. Our efforts resulted in a meeting with Governor Cuomo on January 13, 1987. This resulted in the appointment of a special prosecutor to supersede the district attorney's authority in this case. Feeling very insecure and inadequate next to luminaries such as Dinkins, NAACP state chair Hazel Dukes, well-known attorney Laura Blackburne, Reverend Calvin Butts of the Abyssinian Baptist church, and above all, my father, I took the time to read up on the powers of the governor with respect to special prosecutors. In the meeting, I pointed out to the governor that under article 4 section 2 of the Constitution, his broad supervisory powers gave him the right to appoint special prosecutors, but the special prosecutors would come under the egresses of the attorney general's office and the special prosecutors themselves would be considered deputized attorneys general. The governor was astonished by my understanding of the issue and suggested that he might hire me. He would take that back as the years would move on.

Immediately after the appointment, the two legislators in the room, Assemblyman Green and myself, decided that we were going to write a hate crimes bill try to get it passed in the legislature. By March 5, 1987, Green and I were among a group of legislators and civic leaders who promoted the passage of this bill and gained national acclaim for our efforts. Other deaths of black men and women, either from the excessive force of the police, or hate crimes perpetrated by other citizens, were haunting the political environment of that era. James Powell, a fifteen year-old high school student who was killed by Police officer Thomas Gilligan in July of 1964, ignited the

Harlem riots. Clifford Glover, a ten-year-old child, who walked his father to the train station on his way to work and was walking back home early in the morning in Queens in 1973, as well as Randolph Evans, shot to death by police officer Robert Torsney while standing on the stairway of his Brooklyn apartment building. This defendant was acquitted when the defense introduced a psychiatric condition not accepted by the American Psychiatric Association but by twelve jurors, infuriating all communities.

These cases, when combined with recent police actions resulting in the deaths of Michael Stuart in 1983 and Eleanor Bumpers in 1985, were compelling lawmakers to take state action. As Governor of the state, Mario Cuomo adroitly wanted to circumvent the anger and frustration that was boiling over in so many communities. He convinced Warren Anderson, majority leader of the New York state Senate, that the legislature had to pass a hate crimes bill. Apparently, Anderson was willing to comply, with the exception, that sexual orientation not be included. The Democratically-led Assembly would pass that bill, but the Republican-controlled Senate was vehemently opposed to the inclusion of sexual orientation as part of the protected classes.

In a bold exhibition of trust, the gay and lesbian communities, later known as the LGBT communities, were willing to let the bill pass without the inclusion of sexual orientation. But in a daring response to this more-than-noble gesture, caucus chair Assemblyman Green, state senator and Brooklyn activist Velma Montgomery, and myself declared that we would not pass a hate crimes bill that had hate as part of its portfolio. In this case, Dr. King's admonition that injustice anywhere means injustice everywhere was favored over his bromide that the *arc of history moves slowly but it bends toward justice*. The hate crimes bill would not pass until the year 2000, thirteen years later. There was a great deal of agitation and criticism over our decision on this matter, but with the distinct advantage of hindsight, I don't think any of us ever regretted the action we took.

Now speaking about this time period, I am reminded of a story.

August 15, 1987:

We were arranging to rename Mt. Morris Park to Marcus Garvey Park in honor of the famous black nationalist leader. Ironically, my grandmother Evangeline Paterson had served as Mr. Garvey's secretary in his Harlem offices during the early 1920s. Many of the community activists in Harlem, the same ones who attended the Anti-Apartheid rally two years earlier—joined by Muhammad Ali—would be included in the ceremony, and we were having a meeting to determine the program. A longtime activist, known as Queen Mother Moore, who was nearly ninety years old, announced that Marcus Garvey had a childhood friend with whom he had communicated through his entire life, and that she would be coming all the way from Jamaica to attend the rally. She also added, that the woman, known as Nurse Anne, was a hundred years old herself.

As circumstance would have it, Nurse Anne was the first member of the committee to arrive at my office this warm August morning. The uniformed nurse was escorted in by my assistant Anna Barrow. Sitting with her in my office, I introduced myself and asked a few questions when she abruptly asked in a pronounced Jamaican accent, "Where are the other members of the committee?"

"They haven't arrived yet, nurse," I responded, thinking it would be great because I would get a chance to know a little bit about Marcus Garvey in his younger years. However, Nurse Anne was having none of it as she summarily scolded me.

"I hope you are aware that I do not sit in a room with a man unaccompanied."

This had been an exciting opportunity for me because at the time I was thirty-three years old and had never met anyone who was over one hundred years of age. I was crestfallen by the implication that I had any designs on Nurse Anne, but conceded to her that I would wait in the lobby for the rest of the guests, rose from my chair, and walked to the door. As I was turning the knob to leave, Nurse Anne had a second mandate.

"Young man, come back and sit down."

Puzzled but patient I complied with her request. She asked, "do you happen to be married, young man?"

"No, I'm not."

She grabbed my hand and said, "Then you can sit next to me."

Well, it turned out that Nurse Anne had quite a sense of humor and she completely enjoyed the achievement of baffling and unnerving her host that day.

DECEMBER 2, 1991:

We got a call from someone who refused to identify himself and, to this day, has not done so. We believe he was an employee of the General Services Administration, which is a federal government agency. He informed us that a $275 million office building that would stand thirty-four stories high was under development in lower Manhattan between Broadway and Duane, Reade, and Elk streets. Excavating for the foundation of this major construction, the builders came across a series of remains and artifacts.

Previous research contended that such remains would not be in this place. It was known that the old negro burial grounds, which existed in early New York from approximately 1710–1795, was probably the original site for these remains. But different types of construction on this site for 196 years should have destroyed any evidence. Only 1 percent of animal or human deaths yield evidence of remains or artifacts and this was not an area, far enough into the ground, to qualify as such a venue. But the caller, who I would later refer to as "deep throat" insisted that this was against regulations and the federal government was going to destroy these valuable remains, adding, "I have contacted over a hundred elected officials and civic leaders and not one person has decided to do anything about it." While I was puzzled by the call, my staff member, at that time, Gina Stahlnecker, interestingly, the only white member of my small district office, suggested that valuable history would be lost if somebody didn't take an action. This suggestion was favored over my original reaction that unless the burial grounds were located in Chicago, helping to preserve the resting place of a bunch of dead people would yield little political value. Pertaining, of course, to the story of dead officials not being taken off the electoral role, hence Charles Wrangle's quote in an interview, "when I die, I want to be buried in Chicago so I can continue to participate in political process.

I always considered the input of my co-workers on issues such as this, and I hope you don't mind if I acknowledge some of them. Anna Barrow, David Finn, Millie Gold, Geoffrey Garfield, Sheila Greene, Eric Huckaby, Jeanique Green, and Woody Pascal served my constituents and handled their emergencies. They made me look more diligent then I really was. Mr. Pascal served as my Chief of Staff in that office and then ran my central staff when I become the Minority Leader of the Senate.

With salary compensation at a minimum, the need for efficient and dedicated staff members required me to find talent that came cheap but would eventually achieve greatness. There were two superstars that emerged from this team. In 1991, Joseph Haslip was wandering around pondering his faith when we hired him to work in our office. He stayed for eleven years, six of them as Chief of Staff, and eventually he became the pension manager for New York City as part of his role working for the New York City Comptroller, William Thompson. He has since tracked roles in hedge funds and in private equity. The lesson is that after hanging out with friends, Joe would go home, put a book under his pillow, and wake up knowing all of the contents, like Edgar Casey.

And then there was Karen Boykin-Towns, who lobbied me on behalf of independent colleges my first year in Albany, 1986. In 1987 she asked for a recommendation for employment pursuant to her graduation from the College of Mt. St. Vincent. When the prospects didn't pan out, she accepted a summer job in our office, pledging to stay for a few months before moving on because "I hate politics," or so she said. She stayed for six years, was my youngest Chief of Staff, eventually leaving at the request of Manfred Ohrenstein, the Minority Leader, to serve as one of his top advisers. She married one of my dear friends, former Assemblyman Darryl Towns, and relocated to the private sector at Pfizer, where she eventually served on the leadership teams of the COO'S, Chuck Hardwick and Rich Bagger. She now consults with Ed Gillespie, one of the great political advisors in our country. In 2018 she was elected Vice President of the National Board of the National Association for the Advancement of Colored People. She remains the author of the greatest understatement that I have ever heard when she took the initial position. So, we began the Task Force for the Oversight of the African Burial Grounds. Nobody seemed particularly willing to be helpful to this cause until we got the Public Buildings and Grounds committee of the subcommittee of the House of Representatives to convene hearings in July of 1992.

At that point we were able to get Congressman Rangel to be the first elected official, other than myself and a few others, to take a stand testifying before that committee. "This is our Ellis Island," Rangel said to the conveners, whereupon Congressman Gus Savage, the chair of the committee, admonished the General Services Administration and had sent William Diamond to preserve the remains that lay in the burial grounds with instructions to discontinue any construction until this was achieved. Mr. Diamond then became somewhat of an advocate for the project, and we discovered that the national historic preservation act which was passed in 1969, contained a provision in section 106 mandating that remains or artifacts were to be preserved during federal construction.

Ironically, this provision was fought for by Jewish activists in lower Manhattan, just blocks away from the African burial grounds, where the old Jewish burial grounds had been destroyed during construction in 1961. These community-minded leaders did not want this fate to befall anyone else, and, but for their actions, we would not have been able to save the African burial grounds.

The remains were sent to Howard University for archaeological study with a great contribution from Dr. Michael Blakey of Howard. The research provided some unparalleled information. Comparisons of the grave site artifacts with native African countries revealed that the remains were from places such as Ghana, Angola, Mozambique, and Nigeria. This was among some of the first positive links that revealed the indigenous countries from which Africans were brutally abducted and brought to this country as slaves, years ago. In a gruesome discovery, 72 percent of the remains that were studied were children, and that the main cause of death was trauma. In a rather surprising development, there was a set of remains that bore the uniforms of the British navy and artifacts from the British navy surrounding them. Upon historical review, we now know that some freed Africans from New York actually chose to fight for the British because they were offering the Africans in the New World, a plan for indentured servitude which could lead to their freedom, as opposed to the brutal slavery that the freedom-loving American colonist hypocrites chose to uphold.

My favorite discovery was that, among the first one hundred remains that were exhumed, ninety-nine of them were facing the west, which was an African tradition. Every time I say this, where it is reported, they say that the remains faced east, but these remains at the African burial grounds were facing west. There was one set of remains that was facing the east and to our shock, archaeological-research identified this set of remains as belonging to a Caucasian, so we were wondering who was this white guy that's buried in the African burial grounds with all the Africans. Maybe it was an old boyfriend of Shirley MacLaine.

But once again, details that escaped me when I was a history major at Columbia, and apparently escaped everyone else, is that in 1741, a white man by the name of Cuffey led a slave revolt in New York City. It is believed that as punishment for his participation in this illegal act, Cuffey was buried with the Africans to shame him for his action. After all the 415 remains were studied, there were six to eight others who were identified as non-Africans in the cemetery. The experience reminds me of the movie, *Glory*, where the white captain of the black platoon was buried with his fellow black soldiers by the Confederates as a punishment for him. At the end of the movie, we read that his family wrote to the federal government, thanking them that their son was buried with, what they described as, those brave black soldiers. It also reminded me of Dr. King, who made sure to point out the white who attended the march on Washington on August 28, 1963. Sometimes when there is racial strife, there becomes a counter-reaction to it, and in that moment, most of the members of the oppressive group become simpatico with what has happened.

Once again it brings me to the postulations of Deepak Chopra:

> In the end, we are all the same, in the end we are all capable of doing what the evilest of us have done, we're also all capable of doing what the most virtuous of us have done. Colors, preferences, and regions only separate us in a physical way, but in the end, we are all the same. Salute the people you admire because you're just like them and learn to love your enemies because you act just like them too.

In 2007, the African burial ground was declared to be a national monument. As Lieutenant Governor of New York, I was part of that ceremony and it's just further evidence of my belief that black history is not only American history, it's American history told more accurately.

SPEAKING OF BLACK history, in retrospect, I could view March 20, 2014 as one of the saddest days of my life, if not the saddest. It was the last day I had a conversation with my dad. I had a number of them during the day from about 1 o'clock in the afternoon until 7:30 when my mother left him and went to dinner. The next day he underwent surgery to install a medical device that would help his heart pump and continue his life for about a year. After the surgery, he had some communication with all of us, but by a week later there was no more, and on April 16th 2014 he died. But in another sense, it was a fantastic day, as my dad was lucid and charismatic and we had conversations about government, politics, sports, and people we knew. My mother was there the whole time and eventually, we were joined by my sister-in-law, Eloise Paterson, and close family friend Kendall Reid. Somewhere between 7:30 and 8:30, we wished my dad well, my mother told him she would be there for the surgery in the morning, and we then went to the restaurant Settepani on 120th Street and Malcolm X Boulevard in Harlem.

Toward the end of the evening, I received a call from a woman named Jung Uhn. Over the past three years, I had worked on some projects with

Jung. I had met her on one of my trips to China the year before, during which, she had introduced me to a gentleman who wanted to start a professional football league in China. As farfetched as this idea might have been, she alerted me in the phone call that she was with the gentleman, whose name was Marty. She believed, if I was to serve on the board of his company, there would be a very good professional relationship for me to establish and she summoned me to meet them at a restaurant in midtown Manhattan. I told Jung about the scheduling of my father's surgery, that I was with my family, and didn't want to leave them, so I suggested perhaps they would come uptown and we could talk for about half an hour.

Remembering that they had a car service, she agreed to come uptown, but then I realized the restaurant we were in had music that evening and it might be difficult to have a conversation. I moved the meeting to a bar and restaurant known as Park West on 112th Street and Frederick Douglass Boulevard, which is the extension of Central Park West and also known as 8th Avenue. Passing this address onto Jung Uhn, I invited my mother, sister-in-law, and our friend Kendall for a nightcap, telling them I had to take care of something but it would only take about half an hour and this might be a relaxing way to end the evening prior to my dad's surgery. Eloise said she'd had one drink and was at her driving limit, Kendall said something about not having any makeup on. My mother didn't seem to say one way or another but, without a car to drive us home I didn't want to be outside late at night trying to hail a cab with my mother and by this time, it had started raining.

So, I had the three women drop me at the Park West establishment before they returned home, where I was confronted with anxiety, as I have so many times when I enter a bar by myself. I have done almost everything else by myself and never had any qualms, but something about a bar, loud music, dark rooms, and intoxicated people, always rubbed me a little bit the wrong way, so when I entered Park West, I gingerly removed a chair from the end of the bar closest to the door and sat alone for about five minutes.

Suddenly, the door of the bar swung open and a very enthusiastic gentleman loped through it, noticed me, and embraced me with a bear hug and a very friendly greeting. "What are you doing these days?" He inquired, and I responded, "I've been consulting," and as he invited himself to sit beside me, I returned the inquiry hoping to determine who this person was since he obviously knew me, and it appeared I knew him but just wasn't recognizing him. He offered that he had a gig right now that ended in June but didn't know what he was going to do then. He invited me to have a drink with him. Now I'm thinking, *is it a recommendation he's looking for, or a job?*

Somehow, his ebullient affection for me seemed to have some motive but I had to concede that I was having such a nice time talking with him that I didn't really mind what he was going to ask me. I was happy to comply with his request. We're now joined by Jung Uhn and Marty. In my three-year interaction with Jung Uhn, I didn't really know anything about her family, whether she was dating or ever been married, only business and potential deals occupied our conversations. I reintroduced myself to Marty, I was somewhat astonished when I noticed Jung was paying attention to my new drinking buddy who sat to my right. When Jung Uhn shook my hand, she was looking right at the gentleman and not even at me! I was flabbergasted. Jung Uhn has a life, Jung Uhn has a pulse, she is a real human being who notices other human beings and this reaction has made my night. Now Jung offers her hand to the gentleman at the bar introducing herself, "Good evening, I'm Jung Uhn" and the gentleman shakes her hand and says, "Good evening, I'm Denzel Washington."

OK, now I am shocked. My brother knew Denzel Washington when they were both attending Fordham University. Of course, Denzel actually starred in the movie *Glory*, which I mentioned earlier. Others that went to Fordham shared their memories of him as well, but I had never met him. I could have revealed that I had been sitting there for the last fifteen minutes talking to one of the greatest actors of this era and had no idea who he was, but I decided not to do that, I decided to, as they say . . . chill.

Marty and Jung talked to Denzel and I'm sitting there, now deciphering that when he was talking about the gig that would end in June, it was his performance in the Broadway play, *A Raisin in the Sun*, and while his gig ended in June, and though he was looking for things to do, he clearly didn't need assistance from me in that regard.

At this point, we were joined by Michael Van, one of Harlem's distinguished residents and a manager of different restaurants all over Harlem and the Upper West Side. He was there to have drinks with Denzel and they moved to the back of the restaurant. Whereupon Jung Uhn turns to me and says, "So Governor, this is your jet-set life? You hang around with Denzel Washington every night?" And, I laughed and chided, "No, no, it's not like that. Denzel and I only get together every couple of months or so."

8

A Seventh Bullet

October 12, 2002:

It was a Saturday and I was hanging around the house in Guilderland when I got a phone call from one of my dearest friends, who was my treasurer at one point as a state senator, and now had joined me in the Senate after his election in 1998. Eric Schneiderman became the head of our campaign committee in the year 2000. We had a motto called "six and change." If we won six Democratic seats, we would become the majority. In the end, we won none of them. In addition, it was widely known that three or four of our members were always providing information to the majority, meaning the Republicans, so not only did we raise 1/10th of the money that they did, but we also had 9/10th of our information transferred to them by traitors in our own conference. This came to a head in January 2001 when a group of us met with Martin Connor, who was the minority leader, to complain about this. Particularly about the late Olga Mendez, who had been an outstanding senator and a great freedom fighter in the Puerto Rican community. But in her spare time, was always endorsing Republicans, like Governor George Pataki for reelection in 1998. Mendez also commanded the third highest bonus, paid to her for being the chair of our conference. Only the deputy minority leader, myself, and the leader, Mr. Connor, received more resources.

The members were refusing to vote for her in a night of drinks that preceded this meeting but basically folded right in front of Senator Connor the next afternoon. Stunned by these gutless performances after a previous evening of such verbosity, I raised my hand to Senator Connor and said, "Marty, I'm going to risk our friendship and these people can speak for themselves, but a lot of members don't want to vote to make someone chair of our conference who regularly disseminates information to our opponents." Senator Connor said "Fine, we don't make her chair of the conference. She then just wanders over and sits with the Republicans." And my response was, "we run against her and beat her. Connor's retort was, "That'll cost us $500,000." I responded, "That's the best $500,000 we'll ever spend because even if we lose, who around here is such a profile in courage that they'll risk getting a primary?" Sometimes even when you lose a fight, the winner never picks on you again. This logic was right out of the profound wisdom of Mr. Miyagi in *The Karate Kid*.

So, we resolved the issue that we would let Senator Connor appoint Mendez as chair of the conference, we wouldn't vote on it even though our bylaws said that we should, no one would object to it. He gets to keep Mendez and we don't have to vote for her. But as we moved into 2002, Senator Connor was getting a lot of flak from the Bronx County leader and a Bronx County state senator, now deceased, named Guy Velella. It appeared the Democrats would never put a candidate up against Velella and in exchange, Velella would share some of his discretionary member item money, meaning money that could be designated by an individual senator to a certain number of not-for-profits in their district and that this would be the tradeoff for him not getting a primary.

Previously in the year 2000, Senator Schneiderman talked Lorraine Coyle Koppell, a noted lawyer, into running against Velella, and though Velella won, it was somewhat of a close race.

To exact revenge in the 2002 reapportionment, meaning that the legislative districts were redrawn, Schneiderman, who represented the Upper West side, was drawn into Washington Heights, which was overwhelmingly Dominican, and David Paterson who was representing that part of Washington Heights, was sent back to the West side so that a Dominican candidate could defeat Schneiderman in the general election. But Schneiderman surprised everyone, not only by winning, but getting 45 percent of the Dominican vote. He also felt that some of the money that went to support Guillermo Linares, was funneled from our Democratic conference and now Schneiderman was making an appeal that we must remove senator Connor as leader if we ever wanted to have a chance to win the majority.

Riding back from a visit in Massachusetts that day, Schneiderman invited me to lunch. We went to a little restaurant on Route 20 in Schenectady. Unlike other times when we had lunch, Schneiderman suggested, since it's the weekend, that we have a glass of wine, we had two.

That's around the time he informed me of all these activities of which I'm not aware. This ends in his plea to me that I should run for minority leader at which point I said, "you must be kidding." Schneiderman reached into his briefcase and took out something that I think would have been more dangerous than a .357 magnum. It was a legal pad with ten names on it. He said, "These people are willing to support you for leader. I listed your name and mine as part of the ten, we need thirteen votes, so I got you to ten. Please get in, get the other three votes, become the leader, and let's start trying to win the majority."

Suddenly I felt encroaching asphyxiation and inebriation at the same time. "Eric," I said, "I've seen these battles before. At first, everybody jumps on board because it seems like fun, let's get rid of the leader, have all new leadership positions, then the other leaders come around the leader because no one likes an insurrection no matter what party they're in, and the coup is quashed." But the erstwhile state senator who represented the Upper West Side and now Washington Heights was not to be deterred. He recruited Joseph Haslip, my former chief-of-staff, to help persuade me and anyone else who had any kind of influence on me. He tried to influence them to get me to change my mind.

SPEAKING OF JOE, I am reminded of a story. I was walking home from my office in the state office building in November, 1994. I got off my stop at 135th Street in Harlem and approached my block on 132nd Street in the bitter cold. I was approached by a small woman that, from the lights of the McDonald's behind us, I could see had a bright red coat and a white pull-over hat. She was an older woman who must have had hard times; she didn't seem homeless or malnourished, but she asked me If I could spare a dollar because she didn't have anything to eat. I complied with her request and took the top bill out of my left pocket and wondered what amount of money it was, failing to remember what the top bill might be, as I keep my money with the larger bills in the bottom. So, knowing that it's half a block from my house and McDonald's being a safe place, I took the bill and held it right up to my eye to look at it. To my surprise, as I handed the woman the money she seemed now unwilling to accept the donation. She said, "I don't think I should do this to you." I realize that as frigid as the temperature, as bluster-ing was the wind, she did not want to take money from a disabled person who might be suffering the same problems she did. "Oh Ma'am," I exclaimed, "I am perfectly capable of giving you this dollar, but because you've demonstrated this character and would forgo the money you need to eat, in favor of someone who might need it more, I must tell you that's as good a demonstration of character that I have witnessed in a long time."

"Thank you, Sir" she said.

"I'd like you to know that you should not presume blind people are not always indigent. I happen to be a very wealthy man and I am going to give you this $20 bill to go and eat wherever you'd like in the neighborhood and wish you the best."

She thanked me profusely and I went on my way. That would have been the end of the story if not for the fact that it appeared that once or twice a week for some time, I kept running into the woman in front of the McDonald's and having pronounced this great supposed wealth, that I didn't have, I had to keep up with the payments. I must have given ten or fifteen $20 bills to her over a period of time. Walking home from the state office building on 125th Street up to 132nd one night, I was with my chief of staff, Joe Haslip, and I said to Joe, you know I haven't seen that woman for a few weeks now. I wonder where she is?"

Joe responded, "I think she retired to Florida on your money."

Now, BACK TO the bigger story. This leads to a dinner on October 19, 2002, between myself and state senator Malcolm Smith at Roth's steakhouse on Columbus Avenue on the Upper West Side of Manhattan. While Schneiderman, Haslip, and others were providing me with the political architecture and how it could be renovated with my victory, Smith took a completely different approach. He asked me why it was so important that I stay the deputy leader and not run for the leader itself. "Because Malcolm, I've watched these things before, people say they are with you and they're not with you, then you're all alone, then in the end, when you lose, they basically take your office and all of your staff and they take the car that you are assigned." Malcolm looked back at me and said, "why do you need a car, you can't even drive?" When we got over the mirth of that moment, he said to me, "you know what I think the problem really is?"

"Tell me, Malcolm, what is the problem?"

"You're the son a very famous man, a great man who's extraordinary on many levels and he is so imposing as leader that you don't see yourself as having any leadership quality at all."

He went on to say, "I've always thought that you operate at half the speed you could. You basically try to get the job done but you never try to do your absolute best because you know it will fall short of your predecessors. Maybe not just your father but people like Percy Sutton as well. David, there comes a time in a person's life when they have to just go out and get something and maybe they don't have everything organized, maybe they're just going on faith, but I think this is your time, and to tell you how much I think of it, if you lose, I'll drive you home every night so you don't have to worry about the car. And by the way, if the emotion of this moment makes you want to cry, it's all right to cry."

"Really?" I replied to Malcolm, and just bringing my hand back, I touched my eyelids, realizing that they had tears on them.

As Malcolm was driving me home, I, for some reason, thought of this silly children's movie that has a major quality moment, the name of the movie is *The Sandlot*. It's about some kids who play baseball and they hit a ball over the fence of the sandlot. A ball that had been given to one of the children by his father and it had been signed by Babe Ruth. The best baseball player of the group has a dream and is encouraged by Babe Ruth himself in the dream to jump over the fence and retrieve the ball, even though there is a giant dog over there that he would have to get past. "There are heroes and there are legends, kid," the imaginary Babe Ruth says. "Heroes die and legends live forever." The kid goes on to become the star player for the LA Dodgers. Now this memory seems too silly to put in this book but it happens to be what I was thinking at that moment, and I decided, maybe this was my moment, and maybe it wouldn't work out, but I was going to go for it.

Of course, just as I predicted, at first it appeared we had more than enough votes, meaning thirteen-plus, to wrest the leadership from Martin Connor, but then the fear game begins because, in the end, you don't want to be on the end of the leader's wrath if you don't kill the king. As an example, let's say a senator close to Marty Connor calls Eric Schneiderman and says, "Eric who are you with in this leadership race?" and Eric says, "David Paterson" and the senator says, "Well who else is with David Paterson?" and Eric says "Malcolm Smith" and the other person starts laughing, "Oh Eric, don't you understand? He's our spy." So, the fear that's promulgated when a leader is in power and the challenger has no power, frequently overwhelms the insurrection.

Sitting in my apartment on the evening of November 12, I explained this to Joe Haslip, who said to me, "well if that's the case then you have to think of something that no one ever thought of before." Thanks, Joe! Maybe

I will reinvent the theory of quantum energy, like the famous physicist Niels Bohr, but how will that help me win the majority? Upon Joe's departure, I started to take his comments seriously. I start to play with ideas as to how I could do something different and win the majority. I keep coming back to one thought. Let's just go for it.

At 11 o'clock at night, I call all thirteen people who have pledged their vote to me and asked them to meet me in my office—in the Harlem state office building—at 1 o'clock on the next day, November 13. One of the members, Martin Dilan, a newly-elected state senator who had been a city councilman and who I had not known previously, said to me, "Listen David, I have to think this over for a couple of days but please let me come to the meeting because I think I would like you to be the leader, but I can't pledge myself to you and please keep that secret."

So, I did. Surprisingly, the other twelve showed up including Neil Breslin who came all the way from Albany, and state senator Byron Brown, who came all the way from Buffalo, New York.

I said "Ok folks, here we are, the thirteen of us are together. This number gives us the majority of the 25 people who will vote. So, there are two ways we can win this election, one, is that we sit in this room for the next six days until the actual vote on November 19, next Tuesday, obviously that's not possible,"

"So," I was asked, "what was the other way?"

"Many of you are not going to like this but if you don't allow me to do this, I'm going to call senator Connor and tell him I withdraw and we'll vote for him as leader next week."

"Ok, David let's hear it."

I said, "I want to hold a press conference." Did you know that when 13 people are cursing at you at the same time, that you can hear all of the words?

So, I responded, "ok, I'll just call senator Connor, we'll end this battle, I just take my licks and we'll move on."

And they said, "Well David why do you need to have a press conference right now?"

I said, "look, if you want me to be your leader, you're going to have to trust me, do you all trust me?"

"Yes we do."

"Well that's good because sometimes, when I negotiate with the other leaders, I may not be able to tell you everything that we're talking about, but

I will have the conference's issues as the top of my agenda, I promise. In fact, I'll start right now. I can't tell you why I have to have a press conference, but if you just trust me, this will lead to me becoming the leader."

The members go in the other room and start signing typed up oaths and rehearsing little statements they're all going to make at the press conference about how they're supporting the new leadership of David Paterson. I, on the other hand, am sitting in the room by myself, knowing that I only have twelve votes because senator Dilan has not yet committed to me, and so I tried a little move.

I called state senator Carl Andrews from Brooklyn, who I basically liked but in this situation was bouncing back and forth like a tennis ball at the US open. He was on everybody's side. When he answered, I said, "Carl, I have the thirteen members, I have the thirteen votes and I'd like you to know that I will be the leader. I'm sorry it didn't work out for you, you won't be on my leadership team, but I'll try to do the best that I can."

Andrews went crazy. "What do you mean? Why didn't you call me?" he shouted. "I'm with you, I've been with you . . ."

"Well carl, unfortunately, twelve other people beat you to the punch. But you know there are still twelve members left, and if you'd like to be in succession, you'd better be here in 45 minutes because we're having a press conference."

"Press conference for what?

"To announce me as leader, so if you don't want to appear on TV don't come. It doesn't matter to me because I already have the votes."

"Oh no. Oh No. Mr. Leader, I'll be there."

He showed up with fellow state senator Velmanette Montgomery from Brooklyn, so now I had fifteen votes. So, senator Dilan, a very honest man, and as great a friend as time would allow asked me to step into the hall.

He said, "David, I really wanted to support you and that's why I came to this meeting, but I see that Carl Andrews is here and I assume that he has signed the oath which would kind of make him the thirteenth member and part of the leadership team. But I'm asking you, if you would, on my word, understand that I just needed time to think about this. I don't know you very well but if you let me sign the oath now and make me the thirteenth member, I swear to you there will be plenty of pressure the next couple of days for me to change my vote and I won't change it."

I believed Dilan, I kept him as the thirteenth vote, Andrews fourteen, Montgomery fifteen and we went and held the press conference. Everybody held up their oaths, everybody spoke, the press conference was over, and I went back to my office and sat back in my chair. After ten seconds of peace and quiet, I was invaded by senators Schneiderman and Smith, basically, my two best friends in the conference.

Malcolm said, "I'm with ya chief, but I have no idea what you're doing."

Eric continued, "yeah David, now Marty knows who all the votes are against him."

"My response was, gentlemen, Marty knew who everybody was in the room because there is so much gossip in this conference that you can't keep any secrets. He knew who was in the room probably before they even got there. And, I'll say this, you're right, people take their word back, they say they're with you then they're not. They take their word back all the time. It's a shame that people in government are that disingenuous but you know something, people can take their word back, but they can't take their picture back, and by tonight, I will have all their pictures on television from Buffalo to Long Island, to Brooklyn, to Binghamton, and all around this state."

My comrades were shocked. I then said, "And another thing, there'll be a sixteenth vote coming out, his name is Seymour Lachman. He didn't know about the meeting and called all upset that I didn't invite him. He will say he accepts the ruling of the fifteen votes and wants to be the sixteenth by tomorrow morning. It's tantamount to the old west, you always have a bullet in your gun that no one knows about.

Six days later I was voted in unanimously as the first non-white legislative leader in the history of New York. About a month later, I got a call from former Assemblyman Mike Bragman. He led a similar insurrection against the speaker of the New York state assembly, Sheldon Silver, back in 1999 that failed. He said to me that somebody had suggested that he stand his members up publicly when he had them, but he didn't do it. He said, "when I watched the genius of your facilitating the media to ensure the honesty of your supporters, I sat there and thought, if I had done that, I could have been the speaker of the New York state assembly."

I never knew that much about Bragman, I was actually a friend of Shelly Silver's, but I realized when he told me this, that senator Malcolm Smith was right, that I really had never given 100 percent of my ability to any task.

In 2015 Senator Smith was convicted of accepting bribes and was sent to prison for seven years. It was really a shame. I don't think Malcolm has a criminal bone in his body but sometimes his judgment got the best of him.

I will always see him as a wonderfully spiritual person and a great advisor to me. He's been a great friend to me and believed in me more than I believed in myself.

Eventually, he'll pay his debt to society, but I don't know if I can ever repay my debt to him and—until recently—State Attorney General, Eric Schneiderman.

9

Being There

August 19, 2008:

The special session of the legislature was underway, to address a $3 billion budget deficit that had accrued four months since the legislature passed a budget. Its commencement was delayed by an ignorant and uninformed op-ed piece written by one of the legislatures contending that the proposal for this special session was misguided. Moreover, the editorial chided my judgment, contending we frequently have budget deficits that arise during the middle of the year, but that we address them at the end of the cycle, as we should, in April 2009.

In fact, between the time I gave the televised address to New York citizens and the special session commenced, the gap had risen to $4.2 billion, which was unprecedented at any point in the state's history. The motives of the author were so revoltingly self-aggrandizing that I will conceal the name of the legislator, but his initials were RORY LANCMAN, an Assemblyman whose ignorance was only surpassed by his obsequious desire to please the speaker of the assembly. In the two-day session, we were able to eliminate about 45 percent of the debt, which was far less than I desired, but it did demonstrate that the legislature answered the call, responded, and we would await further data from our budget analysts.

Inevitably, the budget deficit that we feared could be as much as $12 billion, turned out to be $21.3 billion. It was the highest escalation of a budget deficit experienced by a state in one year in the history of this country. Though New York State had far fewer financial issues than California, Illinois, Arizona, and the like, during that particular time, we were the hardest hit by the 2008 economic crisis, because it was mostly a Wall Street profit crisis. New York State derives approximately 22.5 percent of its revenues from Wall Street. The second state in terms of that source of revenue generation is New Jersey with 9 percent and Connecticut third with 8 percent.

Later in the year, on December 16, I would become the first governor of the state to actually issue his 2009–10 budget, a month and a half prior to statutory compliance, to give us a head start on trying to address this massive economic crisis.

Somehow, despite fighting off the Republican notion that we were misestimating the revenues we would receive, and the equally-appalling misconception by Democrats that you can close any budget gap by taxing the rich, we passed that budget on time in 2009. The media continued the notion that this was a "chicken little" special session because it really wasn't that important, and it didn't have to happen at that time, and it really was an overblown attempt by a governor to be an alarmist rather than a leader, so they said.

And then came September 14 and 15, 2008, a Sunday night and a Monday morning when Lehman Brothers went out of business, Merrill Lynch was subsumed by Bank of America, AIG was about to go out of business, and Bear Sterns was hanging by a thread. The market was dropping by hundreds of points each day. JP Morgan and Morgan Stanley were considering a possible merger to save themselves. For some reason, Senator John McÇain pronounced that the economic structure and the economy were basically strong. So much for his presidential campaign.

Late in the afternoon of Monday, September 15, I received a phone call from Governor James Doyle of Wisconsin. I had met the governor at two national governor's association meetings and he took a very different approach than the other governors who were welcoming me. He said, "You know, a lot of things happen in a period of time when you've suddenly assumed higher office and if you ever want to discuss any of these problems, just give me a ring because I'd really like to be of help." It was quite a gesture and in the midst of all this conflict, I welcomed his phone call. He informed me that Travel Guard insurance company, which was an AIG subsidiary, was located in Stephens Point, Wisconsin. He said that it was the largest of the bondholders of the state and if it were to fail, as AIG was about to, that the state of Wisconsin would come close to going into default. He said that the secretary of the Treasury, Hank Paulson, had said on CNBC that he was not going to adhere to the business theory that some companies are, as they say, too big to fail, and he asked me to get in touch with Secretary Paulson and inform him that

Wisconsin and many other states could be in some real trouble if AIG went down immediately.

As for the company itself, they had contacted my office on Friday, September 12, to let us know that they would like to access $20 billion dollars of resources from their subsidiaries to address some debt that they had. It needed the approval of the New York state insurance department to do so and when we surmised that we might be able to do this, they expanded the need by requesting an addition $20 billion, making it a total of $40 billion. By Tuesday, September 16, we were talking $60 dollars and I contacted Tim Geithner, who was the head of the Federal Reserve Bank of New York, to apprise him of this serious consequence. Governor Doyle was unsuccessful in his efforts to inform the treasury department of the potential plight of Wisconsin residents, but Secretary Paulson returned my call and gave me the same admonition about too big to fail and reminded me that it was usually Democrats who opposed this concept. I agreed with the secretary's general premise but urged him to consider the difference between the collapse of Lehman Bros and AIG which insures homes and cars and school districts and all sorts of entities, that its tentacles reach so far into American society and culture that we don't know what the ramifications of AIG failing might be and if the administration was continuing to allow AIG to go out of business, that I would have to oppose it publicly.

To my absolute shock, by the next afternoon, I was informed that a press conference would be held, whereby $85 billion dollars would be made available to ameliorate the plight of the insurance company. That number would climb to over $140 billion in the coming months. I was invited to thank the administration for its work—which I was all too happy to do—in a press conference which I held after their press conference.

All of a sudden, the combination of my warnings about the impending financial crisis and my participation in the rescue of AIG, launches me on a media tour to talk about financing, budget problems, economics, and budget deficits of forty-eight of the fifty states. I felt like a novice walking on a high wire because I just felt I didn't know enough about the subject matter to really garner this much attention and people were actually listening to me. One time on CNBC I was making a comment on credit default swaps, one of the tools that landed us in the huge mess that we wound up experiencing. I'm sitting there thinking, all they have to do is ask me what a credit default swap is and I'm dead.

Years later, I was having lunch with a well-known economist, Nouriel Roubini, also known as Dr. Doom. I told him this story and he said "David, the reason they didn't ask you the question is that nobody on Wall Street knew what credit default swaps were, so basically, anything you said would have gone unchallenged." In an article written by the *Wall Street Journal*, after a meeting I had with them on September 30, 2008, they reported that "David Paterson seems to be the only politician in this country who seems to understand the economy." I didn't know if the spirits had bestowed a certain economic genius on me that I didn't have before or if I was in a remake of the Peter Sellers movie, *Being There*.

Suffice it to say, I was on a roll. On Wednesday morning, October 15, I got a phone call from the well-known and revered public relations expert, Howard Rubenstein. He informed me that he had just seen a poll that my approval rating was 64 percent and that my name recognition was 97 percent up, from something like 4 percent earlier in the year. I marked this moment as the apex of my gubernatorial service because, within a couple of hours, I went to an event in lower Manhattan, where I was greeted by my secretary, Charles O'Byrne. It seemed odd that Charles would attend this particular event but when we rode back to the office in a police vehicle, he informed me that the *New York Post* reporter, Fred Dicker, had alerted him that he was aware that Charles had not paid his taxes for a number of years and the money was still due. O'Byrne had talked to me about this in December 2006, right before I took office as lieutenant governor, and made him my chief-of-staff. I said to him that Governor Spitzer was doing background checks on all the employees and that the background check would give us an idea of how serious the matter was, and we would then know how to address it. I also mentioned to Governor Spitzer that there could be a problem and he agreed we should wait until the background checks were completed.

In 2007, as Governor, no background checks came back about any of my employees, and I never thought about the issue ever again. But apparently, O'Byrne did, because he had a meeting with the chief of the state police in May of 2008 and wanted the superintendent whose name was Harry Corbett, to confirm that this issue was no detriment to his service. Later, the superintendent denied that he gave that assurance, it didn't go unnoticed, that neither of the gentlemen bothered to tell me about the meeting or that the issue was still in existence. Furthermore, I became aware that O'Byrne knew that Spitzer was scheduled to resign two and a half hours before the phone call between myself and the governor's secretary, Richard Baum, and didn't tell me, so I guess he sort of forgot who he was working for.

This is a good lesson for all people who are in these staff positions. They often become reverent or intimidated by higher authorities, but miss the fact that your boss has to know everything that you know, or you're no good. Nonetheless, Dicker agreed not to print the story until we could come up with an explanation for why O'Byrne should be serving in the governor's office.

In the office that Wednesday afternoon, we were joined by the first deputy secretary to the governor, Sean Patrick Maloney, and a few other staff members. We learned that only a third of the staff members in the governor's office actually had background checks, and O'Byrne was not one of them. Hustling and searching for an answer, and unknown to me, Friday morning's *Albany Times Union* printed the story about O'Byrne's tax problems. I received a call from Sean Patrick Maloney at 4:00 PM on Friday afternoon, asking me to contact Fred Dicker, who was imploding as only Dicker can, over the fact that the *Times Union* had printed the story before he received an explanation why O'Byrne was working in the governor's office.

Having had a good rapport with Dicker, and honestly believing that in spite of some obstreperous thing he'd written about me on occasion, I knew that in a private conversation, I could apologize for the fact we hadn't given an explanation in time. But that wasn't the reception I received when I made the call. He was unravelling about the fact, and swore on his personal oath to God, that the only time he ever did that to me, and maybe the only time he ever did it in his life, that there was no way the *Times Union* could have printed this story because the source would never have spoken to the *Times Union*. It's the only time a reporter ever said to me, "If you knew who the source of the story was you would know why the story would have come to me and not to the *Times Union*." And somehow, despite my protestations, I could fathom he was telling the truth.

Saturday's *New York Post* obliterated O'Byrne. The other media institutions stepped up their inquiry. In a conversation on Sunday, October 19, my press secretary, Reesa Heller, told me this story is not going away. O'Byrne resigned as secretary to the governor on Friday, October 24, but the incident unleashed an avalanche of negativity directed at me, similar to the first moments in which I became governor.

At this point, my fortunes took a dramatic turn because of very poor judgment on my part. I had a tantrum with Reesa Heller over the phone around that time—who admittedly was very sympathetic—reminding her that the day Michelle and I had to confess to our extramarital activities, that after the press conference, not one staff member came in to the room to ask us how we were doing, if we needed anything, and when we came out of the room, no one said anything to us with exception of a woman named Shammeik Barat, but, when O'Byrne got in trouble for the tax issue, members of the campaign staff came to a meeting to try to help him get out of this mess, which was against regulations.

In addition, it was now clear to me that the *Times Union* got the story from our office in an attempt to get the story written in a more objective fashion than we thought the *Post* would write it. And then, when the plot predictably blew up in everybody's face, who got sent in to try to calm down Dicker? Me, the one who got set up for that quixotic mission. My adjustment to this situation was ill-conceived and generated devastating ramifications. Still reeling from the games that were played with me as I approached my inauguration, this calamity manifested my greatest anxieties and hurled me into a defensive posture. More and more, I surrounded myself with assistants who were loyal and protective, but launched way over their heads in terms of decision-making capacity and judgment. And what a bad time for this to happen, because a monsoon was coming. One that was more devastating for me than the budget crisis and it was called an open US Senate seat.

10

Those Kennedys

November 4, 2008:

Barack Obama is elected President of the United States to the absolute surprise of most Americans and the absolute shock of black Americans, who didn't think we would see this spectacle for another three decades. Robert F. Kennedy, in 1966, made a statement as US senator from New York, that he thought a black person, who at the time he said would be a black man, would become president in about forty years. It was forty-two years, but the senator was essentially right. When I went to the polls, my poll being at 134th Street and Adam Clayton Powell Boulevard, at PS 175 in Harlem, I saw lines completely down the street. I was given an opportunity to go to the head of the line but chose to stand in the back to wait an hour and a half to vote because, I had dreamed of seeing lines at the polls at 11:30 in the morning, as there was that day.

That evening, I appeared on NBC news with Mayor Rudolph Giuliani, and at one point, even though we were both being interviewed, I asked him, "even if you were supporting Senator McCain—who everybody respects—aren't you pleased, as an American, to see that this country could elect a man, whose lineage, for the most part, were slaves brought to the US, and now, one of them, after the emancipation and the civil rights movement, has become president?" He said he agreed.

But after that wonderful day, two weeks passed, at which time, two separate events occurred that would further complicate my life. One was that my poll numbers that were 64 percent approval rating had now dropped to 49 percent. The strange thing was that, during that period, I hadn't done anything that was even controversial or had any missteps or adventures with the media. The only thing that had happened in that time was that President Obama got elected. Also, Malcolm Smith, who was the minority leader of the Senate, became the majority leader because the Democrats took more votes in the statewide elections than the Republicans. The privilege of there being three prominent African American men in leadership positions—from President to governor of New York, and the majority leader of the New York state Senate—all of whom, surprisingly, had wives named Michelle, might not be going over too well in all quarters. President Obama would find that out when, right before his inauguration, a meeting of Republican House and Senate members, designed to embarrass him and cause his administration grief, became known by the public, to the disappointment of the participants. The other complicating element during that time was that President Obama had asked Hillary Clinton to serve as Secretary of state and Hillary Clinton now accepted it, opening up Robert F. Kennedy's former Senate seat.

It is the Governor's choice to fill the unexpired term of the senator, or at least for two years, when the next statewide election would be held, and everybody and their mother wanted to serve in that capacity. And, as if this rapidly-cascading drama needed any more current, on December 2, 2008, I received a phone call at my home that evening from Caroline Kennedy saying that she might be interested in being a candidate. We agreed to keep the conversation to ourselves but by Friday, December 5, ABC news was reporting that Caroline Kennedy was going to be a candidate. I immediately called Caroline and said, "I thought we were going to keep this a secret" and she went over the names she had spoken to and the only one she couldn't vouch for was her cousin, Robert F. Kennedy Jr. whose meddling would continue until this process unfolded.

I released my 2009–2010 budget on December 16, 2008. After the budget presentation that we'd worked hard to submit five weeks before it was due, all the questions were about Senate candidates and 90 percent of them were about Caroline. Counterbalancing this hysteria was the fact that, probably the most qualified person to succeed Hillary Clinton in the Senate was Andrew Cuomo—now serving as the attorney general and with great experience in Washington and in New York State, also, at one point, married to Kerry Kennedy, another of the late senator's eleven offspring. Congressman Gerald Nadler, whose understanding of government is nonpareil, former Congressmember and district attorney Elizabeth Holtzman, Congresswoman Carolyn Maloney, and American Federation of Teachers head Randi Weingarten were just some of the notables who were making themselves available for the position.

Also, dominating the discussion, was the possibility that Malcolm Smith, who should have the votes to make himself majority, might stay in the minority because three senators, Pedro Espada, Hiram Monserrate, and Carl Kruger—known as the three amigos, but who would later be known as the three inmates because they all ended up in prison—had collaborated with a fourth state senator, Rubén Díaz Sr., to perhaps move and sit with the Republicans, restoring their majority. I was able to negotiate with them and keep them on the Democratic side of the aisle, but I surmised that this agreement was temporary and vulnerable, so, when Mayor Bloomberg sat down with me in late December and proposed to me that I appoint myself to the Senate, I told him that I thought it was irresponsible. With there being no lieutenant governor, the next person in line—the majority leader of the Senate—is technically the acting governor not fully assuming the role of governor, as the lieutenant governor does under the law. With these four rather lacking-in-credibility senators, bouncing back and forth like a ping-pong match, it wasn't clear, if I appointed myself, who would take my place, and if that was the case, it would rightly be blamed on me for jumping ship to save myself and subjecting the state to an unconscionable bonfire of the vanities over who would become my successor. The mayor shrugged it off and said, "that's not your problem, you can appoint yourself senator."

SPEAKING OF MICHAEL Bloomberg, a story has come to mind involving Michael, Chris Christie, myself, and the Queen of England. I know, it sounds like the start of a joke but this really did happen.

It was July 8, 2010, and we were lining up to greet the Queen at the reflection pools at the World Trade Center site where she was coming to lay a wreath. Because the World Trade Center site is under the governance of the Port Authority, in official ceremonies, the protocol states that the highest level of authority is the two governors. I was standing in line behind Christie while we waited for her majesty. Chris turned to me and said;

"I was told by the protocol people that nobody escorts the Queen but Prince Phillip, but I bet you that Bloomberg is going to try to stand in front of us both and escort her."

"Yeah, Chris, Michael always takes charge like that. I'm ok with it."

"Well, I'm not putting up with it this time. If he tries it today, I want you to trip him and I'm gonna sit on him."

Christie was pissed. It was 98 degrees and he practically had steam coming out of his ears. I was watching Michael approach and looking at Christie and laughing, and in all this activity, I didn't notice that Her Majesty was standing in front of me trying to shake my hand. Now, I was told by the protocol people that nobody touches the queen so when she touched my shoulder to get my attention, I jumped back thinking I had breached protocol. I regained my composure and said, alluding to the excessive temperature, "your majesty, I know you were expecting a warm reception but this is superfluous." She laughed with me and I could feel Christie's temperature rising again. I think it's the Napoleonic New Jersey syndrome. But we won't go into that.

ON NEW YEAR's Day, 2009, there was a sudden turn of events when the mayor's deputy, Kevin Sheekey, wrote an op-ed article on page two of the *Daily News* saying, "if I don't appoint Caroline Kennedy, who is a friend of the mayor's, it would be, as he termed it, political malpractice."

In retrospect, here is where my zeal and purpose—evident when I convened a legislative session in August in the middle of an election year and vacation period, or when I quashed any meeting with anybody who thought they had the power to stop me from becoming governor—became unwieldy. I did not respond to this public challenge to me about who I had to appoint as a senator and, because of that, the disrespect and public nuisances caused by supporters of different candidates, became a problem.

Stuart Appelbaum, a union leader who's had a for-sale sign on his head for twenty years, wrote a vicious and inappropriate statement about Caroline Kennedy. Meanwhile, reports were coming from Washington that the Kennedy crew are telling people to get on this train now or you'll never get on it, as if they had already made the decision and dictated it to me. In a conversation I had with the late Senator Ted Kennedy's wife, Vicky, she scolded me that this decision should have already been made. Frankly, it astonished me that she would say that. Rumors of promises that I had made, and decisions that have already been vetted, were all over the place. The level of advice and counsel was really poor, and I had not yet found replacements for some high-caliber people who had worked with me in the Spitzer administration but had chosen to leave. One figure that did stand tall and strong during that time was a campaign communications director that we hired by the name of Judy Smith.

She was fighting back against these interferences and was advising me to do the same. As my plane was landing on January 21, 2009, after attending President Obama's inauguration, I got another phone call from Caroline

Kennedy. Caroline had assured me the week before that she was in the race to stay and wanted to be a US senator. Now she was telling me that she did not want to be considered. I asked her why and she said she couldn't tell me, that it was private, and she'd arrived at the decision about fifteen minutes before. Not wishing to talk to her in front of four or five other people, I called her back when I got home and asked her what was going to be the explanation for her departure and she said she didn't have one. I said "well that's going to spark all types of rumors and conjecture as to why this occurred. What you could do," I said, "is just don't say anything and I just won't appoint you." That would have been a good decision for most people, but not for the Kennedys. They must always be number one and by 5:30 that afternoon there was an announcement that Caroline Kennedy was getting out of the race.

I was meeting with staff and advisors that evening and could not reach her the whole time after this announcement was made. While Caroline was radio silent, Bobby Kennedy Jr., went back to the media to make some statements about what he knows I'm going to do or something or other. I called his sister Kerry to complain about this and he called me back to say that he's on a flight to Nova Scotia and won't be bothering me anymore. Fortunately, he kept his word. But at 10:45 PM Caroline reappears, calling me, and I'm asking her why she announced she was getting out of the race, putting the press release out without telling me. She asked me what I wanted to do, and I said, "well, why don't you just put yourself back in the race and I'll handle it unless you want to spend a long time trying to explain your conduct over the last six weeks." She agreed and did put the statement out but it was then reversed two hours later and she now had officially withdrawn from the race. The situation was so confusing that when I called Senator Chuck Schumer to talk about who the possibilities were at 7:00 am—he was one of my advisors—he said he thought that Caroline was out of the race. He was right because I went to sleep before the second announcement that she was out, occurred, and didn't realize she was out of the race until about 10 o'clock that morning.

Following Caroline Kennedy's exit, then reentry, then final exit, and the media's false assertion that she was the choice in this matter, I was informed by Judy Smith, that the media was writing that I must reassess the candidates and offer a runner-up appointment which is making me look bad. My response to Smith was that this was a one- or two-day story and that the appointment will of course, be made by me, and the appointee will be the senator and this will all go away. But Ms. Smith, who had been monitoring the Kennedys' activities, claimed that, in Washington, they were basically telling people that "this train is moving, either get on board or we'll remember it but this disrespect for the process, and me in particular, had to be addressed." "Fine," I said, "then go ahead and address it." Ms. Smith's retort was to mention some minor issues which had come up in Ms. Kennedy's background check, which I told her were unnecessary to address at this point, but we agreed that she would go to battle with the media about the way the appointment was being made. Ms. Smith then commanded a member of my press office, Errol Cockfield, who was not the press secretary, to leak to the *New York Post* that Ms. Kennedy had had an affair with Arthur Sulzberger, the publisher at the *New York Times*. Cockfield has since said that he disputed with Ms. Smith that this was not the right thing to do, but, he eventually did it anyway.

Smith did not tell me, nor did she tell anyone else, nor did anyone know where she got this information, that she believed Caroline Kennedy was having this affair. Cockfield had come back to me about a month before about something else Smith had wanted to do which I intervened to stop, but this time, Cockfield went ahead and leaked this information to the *Post* who had it up by 4 o'clock in the afternoon and when it was reported to me by Charles O'Byrne, my first thought was "Oh My God. Time to die."

I hired Ms. Smith on becoming Governor at the urging of my lifelong friend and now consultant, Lisa Davis. But in checking up on the work she did, Charles O'Byrne pointed out that she was a flamethrower and one who got into these nasty fights, including defending the performer Chris Brown after his assault on another performer, Rhianna. When O'Byrne resigned and there continued to be difficulties with the press office, I thought it best to hire Ms. Smith who was very loyal, very strong, and up until this point, I thought was the most professional person I had. She certainly had my ear. When the story broke in the *New York Post*, O'Byrne called to tell me about this and I was shocked that this had gone on. Now Smith was referring that this story had a few days of life before going off into the wind but I knew that this was a crucible for me, for my office, and for any future campaign.

The issue also overshadowed the appointment of Kirsten Gillibrand, the Congressmember from the capital region, whom I believed was not the best candidate to serve for that year or the next year, but I was sure that ten years out she would be superior to all the other choices. At 42, she was the youngest of all potential candidates, in a year when for the first time, young people between the ages of 18–21 came out to vote. There had been a constitutional amendment passed in 1972 allowing 18-year-olds that privilege but it had never been exercised to any great extent. I thought Andrew Cuomo could step right in, but providing I got an appropriately qualified candidate, I wanted to appoint a woman. I had also considered Randi Weingarten, the head of the America Federation of Teachers, and a couple of others. Gillibrand was my choice and her representation of upstate New York ensured upstaters that they would have a senator that was physically from upstate New York, which they had not had since Charles Goodell was appointed to fill the Senate seat when former-senator, Robert F. Kennedy, was assassinated in 1968.

There was one other reason I liked Senator Gillibrand and it's not fair to the other candidates, but I will explain it. The Congresswoman came to my office on the afternoon of Sunday, December 7, 2008, for an interview. Before the interview started, my press secretary, Risa Heller, read me a press release that we were going to issue after an unflattering and discriminatory caricature was presented of me the evening before on *Saturday Night Live* by the comedian Fred Armisen. The press release said basically "funny skit, nice try," something like that, and offered that I would come on and appear for myself as a solution. I was not happy with this response. At the time there were 37 million disabled people in the United States. Those who were blind had an unemployment rate of 69 percent even though their educational performance was 3 percent higher than the national average. Those with ambulatory disabilities were a little under 50 percent, and 90 percent of deaf people have no jobs. These sarcastic stereotypes were only notions of fear and anxiety that caused the general population to be uncomfortable around the disabled people, let alone hire them. I was not going to yuk-it-up with *Saturday Night Live* just to come on the show and further promote these ignorant stereotypes.

Gillibrand heard the exchange with my press secretary and me and we agreed to talk about it further after the interview. As the interview was coming to an end, Congressmember Gillibrand said to me, "Can I say something? and of course, it's not my business" and then urged me to maintain my stand and fight for people who didn't have a voice, and that although it was all done in fun, there is always a subliminal effect that repeated instances like this have on most who would watch it. Here again, I wa feeling this distance from people who worked for me who would never seem to understand the feeling that I had when *New York Post* reporter Fred Dicker said,

"Incidents like this could really hurt someone's career. Why? They didn't do anything politically, they didn't make a bad decision, they didn't get caught in some kind of scandal, they were just made fun of on a comedy show."

That particular day, Congressmember Gillibrand's voice was one of support and encouragement, and on that day, perhaps all of the other candidates may have agreed, but she was the one that was there, and in the world of coincidence, we're all human beings, but I think I can remember it when I made the choice. It wasn't the sole reason I made the choice, but it was a contributing factor.

The misadventures of the actions taken by people working in my office overshadowed my nomination of Kirsten Gillibrand to become the successor to Hillary Clinton and the fiasco-ignited reprisals from the Kennedy family, the *New York Times*, the general press corps, and even the public.

It turns out, that while the political insiders were sniping at Caroline, the public still loved her. The fact that we were asking the legislature to make more and more cuts and now asking New York's wealthiest to contribute to this $21.3 billion remedy that we must find for the hole in our budget, created a declining confidence in our efforts. But sometimes, from a deep cavern of despair, and a rising climate of anxiety, there is yet a miracle.

11

Presidential Affairs

January 14, 2009:

I'm meeting with a group of women who want to talk about my nomination to the United States Senate. Interestingly enough I spent the first half of the meeting being quite unkind to Caroline Kennedy, who last time I checked, was a woman, but in their view, this was a famous woman and a legacy, and they didn't think that was a great idea. So, I now realize this was not a meeting to convince me to appoint a woman, but it is a meeting to tell me to appoint a specific woman. I never found out who that woman was because I was interrupted to hear that a plane had gone down in the Hudson River. At that point, my press secretary, Risa Heller and I, thought that the plane had crashed into the Hudson and that there would likely be no survivors. Rushing to the west side from 40th Street and 3rd Avenue, where the Governor's New York City office is located, we learned that the plane did not crash, but that it landed in the water and all the passengers had been evacuated safely.

We proceeded to a building right by the Hudson River, all the way over by the West Side Highway and to my surprise, within a couple of minutes, I was standing with a group of people who had just been in a near-fatal plane crash but had survived. Many of them were in such a state of shock that the impact of this amazing rescue may not have sunk into them fully. Some were understandably emotional, but none of them seemed to be particularly stressed out or traumatized from what was almost the last event in their lives.

There was one passenger, however, that I will never forget. I walked up and shook his hand, I believe his name was John and he said to me, "I missed you at the Alcoa press conference on Monday." I had held a press conference for one of Alcoa's ventures in St. Lawrence County, New York.

"You missed me at the Alcoa press conference on Monday?" I just couldn't believe he said it. He proceeded to tell me he was an executive at Alcoa and he was supposed to be there but couldn't get back from another business trip in time and he was sorry we couldn't get together. "You were just in a harrowing plane landing in the Hudson River, nearly submerged, get off the plane and hang around on raft until a cruise boat picks you up, it's freezing cold outside and all you can say is you wanted to apologize to me for not attending the press conference at Alcoa on Monday?"

"Yeah, I really wanted to be there and just couldn't make it work," he said.

"You are just an amazing person," I said.

Approximately five years later, I was on a conference call with executives from Alcoa and, I can't remember what the reason was, but at the end of the conference call, I reminded them of the incident and they named the executive and said, "Yeah, that's just like John."

Mayor Bloomberg joined me at the rescue center and we then held a press conference. Mayor Bloomberg spoke first, and I opened my remarks by saying, "We've had *The Miracle on 34th St.* Now we have *The Miracle on the Hudson*." For about two days I was given credit for this, but this is now a famous expression and a movie whose author has remained nameless, except for an interview prior to the movie where Tom Hanks mentioned that I had offered these remarks. That accolade from him is more important than all the times that my contribution was omitted. That miracle was a flicker of resilience for me, only to be returned to the massive debacle which was the nomination of the United States senator.

REELING FROM THE aftermath of the Kennedy debacle, I arrived on February 2, 2009 to the Council on Foreign Relations, to present my views on the US economy and my belief that public and private capital had to play more of a role in ameliorating these financial issues rather than these G7 and G8 worldwide conferences that didn't include the actors who are involved in this current financial crisis. In the press conference that followed, malicious castigation of my blindness raised its ugly head again. I was informed that union local 1199 Service Employees International Union put out a television commercial with a blind man complaining about how I had turned my back on the blind community through the budget cuts proposed for the 2009–10 budget. A *New York Post* editorial entitled "The Governor's Eyes," from October of 2008 claimed that now Charles O'Byrne had left, there was no one to read to me, obviously forgetting about the 200,000 other state employees who were still there.

Another *New York Post* article advised my staff that they should take me down to the World Trade Center so that I could touch the buildings and learn we have already started building at the site. This in response to a statement I had made that we will be building at the World Trade Center. There was a beginning of construction, but my point was, that after seven years of inactivity, we were going to get this whole project completed in a short period of time. The invitation for my staff to have me visit there was a dig that I could not "see" that the new buildings were in progress.

The National Federation of the Blind picketed NBC and wrote some very strong statements about my treatment in the *Saturday Night Live* episode. NBC had six other scripts using Fred Armisen portraying me as this Mr. Magoo character. September 25, 2010, I finally went on the show and had the last word, saying "you made so much fun of me for being blind, that I forgot I was black."

In March of 2009, I began to rally both emotionally and physically. I brought in a new secretary, Larry Schwartz, who had been the chief-of-staff to Andrew Spano, the Westchester County executive, and replaced a few other staff and campaign people including Judy Smith. She went on to inspire the TV series, *Scandal*, in which Kerry Washington plays a similar press advisor to a president.

Somehow, someway, the majority leader Dean Skelos, Speaker Sheldon Silver, and I, were able to pass a budget that alleviated $21.3 billion of deficit, over $16 billion more than the original projection in 2008, and not including the $2 billion we reduced from the budget when we went into special session in August. The conservatives told me to cut the budget and I did. Progressives told me to tax the rich and I did. Any single way that we could find money to get out of this mammoth, unprecedented hole, we accomplished, and surprisingly, the budget was only one day late and that was because a senator, Ruth Hassel-Thompson, was ill. We didn't have her vote until she returned on April 1.

My poll numbers started to rebound from a 19 percent approval rating. We were looking forward to a smooth end to the legislative session when on June 8, 2009, crisis struck again. The Democrats had a 32–30 majority, a very slim margin in the Senate, and of course, those three or four amigos who had threatened to switch party lines or at least vote for the Republican as the majority leader were still vulnerable. But out of nowhere, around 2 o'clock in the afternoon, while I was delivering a speech in Syracuse, a Republican member called for a vote as to who would be the majority leader. The acting floor leader at the time, Neil Breslin, who was rarely coherent, was a deer in the headlights as two Democrats, Senator Pedro Espada from the Bronx, and Hiram Monserrate from Queens, voted for Skelos, now making him the majority leader, and the Democrats left the floor. Four hours later, Malcolm Smith, who was now deposed as the majority leader, held a press conference announcing that he and the opportunistic senators were all friends. The media was shocked by this response. He said, "It sounds strange but it's actually true." It still sounds strange. I use the word opportunistic because Pedro Espada, a flashy, well-dressed but otherwise vapid personality who lived ten miles from his own district was immediately voted the majority leader of the Republican Senate even though he was a low-level member of the Democratic majority.

This prompted a seventeen-day stalemate where neither side could hold a session because Senator Monserrate, whose "grass is always greener" fence-jumping, had now gone back to the Democrats, meaning that each side now had thirty-one members and could not hold a quorum. Therefore, we couldn't finish the legislative session.

In Albany, the assembly left, they had completed their business, and I couldn't even get these senators all to come into the room at the same time. I offered to preside, as I had as lieutenant governor, and we could vote in a lot of non-controversial bills that provided financial aid to localities who sorely needed it in each of their districts. During this time, my alert counsel, Peter J. Kiernan, went back and spoke with an incredible legal mind, David Nocenti, who had been counsel to Governor Spitzer and did serve with me for the first few months of my term. He'd also talked to previous governors' counsels, going back to Judah Gribetz, who was counsel to Governor Hugh Carey, who served from 1975–1982, and Bob Douglas, who had served as counsel to Governor Rockefeller, who served from 1959–1973 when he was appointed vice president by President Gerald Ford. They all believed that the Constitution never spoke about how to replace a lieutenant governor. But in a 1940s case in the New York Court of Appeals, which is its highest court, directed a Governor to appoint an Attorney General as the previous Attorney General had passed away shortly after assuming office.

All of these gentlemen agreed we had a good chance to break the tie procedurally by me appointing a lieutenant governor and, either way, it would resolve two hundred years of controversy as to whether or not this could be accomplished. I did not want to appoint a political figure, I wanted to appoint someone who was a government or civic leader, pretty much unaffiliated, and arrived at the choice of Richard Ravitch, the former head of the Metropolitan Transit Authority. He was an unsuccessful candidate for mayor in 1989, but only received 6 percent of the vote so I didn't see him as a political figure. We also agreed that he would serve through my term which ended in 2010 and that, on running for reelection, I would choose another lieutenant gubernatorial candidate.

I appointed Ravitch on Wednesday, July 8, 2009. The day before, Andrew Cuomo, the Attorney General, issued a statement that it was his legal opinion that a Lieutenant Governor could not be appointed by the governor and pronounced that I do not make that choice. The Attorney General's memorandum was hurried and cursory at best. I paid it no mind and went ahead with my appointment, but when I informed the attorney general who the appointment was, he seemed relieved. I surmised because it was not Tom Suozzi, the former county executive of Nassau County, someone whom Cuomo deeply despised.

Even prior to the Court of Appeals upholding my right to make the appointment, Pedro Espada ended his shortest term as majority leader and went back to the Democrats and the Democrats replaced leader Smith with Senator John Sampson. Malcolm Smith was a wonderful friend of mine, but he was convicted of an offense and I totally understand that he had to face the consequences. But the catastrophe that ended in him losing his position as majority leader began when Espada asked for $750,000 of discretionary spending, known as a member-item, for a not-for-profit. However, Espada wouldn't describe the not-for-profit's purpose. Smith, fearing that this was an attempt to hire family members or basically launder money into other hands through a not-for-profit, declined the request. Whereupon Espada went to Monserrate and, in cahoots with former gubernatorial candidate Tom Golisano and a lawyer appropriately named Pigeon, hatched a plot to overthrow Smith.

The most galling effect of this transaction is they all got up on camera the day of the coup and said that this was a good government movement. Eventually, three of the four were charged with corruption and Golisano moved out of state. I extend him the kindest wishes from the furthest distance.

My poll numbers were now up 50 percent, into the high 20s as we spent the summer and the fall preparing for the next difficult budget, a $10.2

billion deficit, and a reelection campaign. But the bad feelings generated by the deep budget cuts were resonating with the special interest groups, unions, and others adversely affected.

On September 14, 2009, Larry Schwartz, my secretary, and I received White House political director Patrick Gaspard. Gaspard was a union organizer for healthcare union 1199 and declined an invitation from me to manage my lieutenant governor campaign in 2006 in favor of Andrew Cuomo's attorney general campaign of the same year. Gaspard apprised the two of us that Rudolph Giuliani was going to be running for governor on the Republican line and that the White House did not think that I could beat Giuliani due to the sagging poll numbers and the disapproval I was receiving from the heavy Democratic special interest contributors for cutting the budget so drastically.

Since the request was coming from, in effect, the President, and even though I had considered announcing a year previously that I wouldn't be a candidate in 2010, I knew this was a mess that had to be cleaned up by someone and I felt compelled to do it. It was on my watch and I would probably suffer the consequences, which was happening now. So, just as we had come to a consensus that I'd get out of the race, I made the statement, "Well as soon as Giuliani gets into the race, I will decline to run." Gaspard seemed shaken by my response. He said, "No we have to get to work now, you have to get out as soon as possible." My response was, "Well how does anybody know that Rudolph Giuliani is even running? Where's this information coming from?" Gaspard proceeded to flood the air with barnyard excrement, contending that in 2008 they knew everything that John McCain was doing and this is how they won the election and they know for a fact that Giuliani is going to be a candidate in 2010.

I did not reveal that I knew the reason why Giuliani would not be a candidate and challenged them to substantiate this speculative assertion. As Gaspard was leaving the room, I said to him, "And when am I going to read about this in the newspaper?" He said, "Oh no, this is a private meeting and we don't expect that this should get out from your side either."

Four days later I was having a dinner with some colleagues who are friends of mine, as we often did, but in this meeting, Congressman Gregory Meeks told me that Rahm Emanuel, former chief of staff to Obama, is complaining about the governor of New York and how he is not cooperating.

Saturday morning, I get a call from the Reverend Al Sharpton to the effect of "what's going on with this idea that you're not running for governor?" So, I know that the White House is now talking, and we make attempts to get in touch with them. Larry Schwartz reached Gaspard at 4 o'clock in the afternoon, whereupon he said that there was no further action on this situation for the time being. But at 11:22 PM on Saturday night, I received a call from Charles O'Byrne informing me that there's a *New York Times* story that President Obama wanted me to step down.

There's a firestorm of activity in the next couple of days as to whether President Obama has the right to interfere in an election for governor of New York state which doesn't have anything to do with the House or Senate majorities, it was just his choice to get involved. Exiting a luncheon, a couple of days later, my wife Michelle was approached by reporters asking her what she thought about the situation. Her comment was that the president had enough things to concern himself with in Washington and the should stop meddling in the business of New York State. My father hit the ceiling! He admonished Michelle that we don't criticize the president. This was a valid point because President Obama's election came as such a shock to so many people and that it occurred so much sooner than anyone would have expected. My father once told me that he wouldn't live to see a black president, and neither would I.

The unfortunate ramification of this white-glove treatment of the black president is that he could pretty much do or say as he wanted without any criticism from the black community, with the notable exceptions of the famous professor, Cornell West and the journalist Tavis Smiley. Several congressional representatives told me that, during his term, President Obama was very negative toward the congressional black caucus and they would have loved to have responded but they knew this was an historical circumstance and that the black community would support Obama.

I was present at a black congressional caucus dinner when President Obama told the forty-six members of the organization that he didn't need them to put on their criticism shoes, he needed them to put on their marching shoes. I was wondering what it was they needed to march about now that he was president. But Michelle's message to the president was supported by 71 percent of the population in polls during that period of time. As a guest on *Meet the Press*, I covered for the president myself by not admitting that they had told me to get out of the race. As soon as the *New York Times* editorial hit, Congressman Gregory Meeks put on his website, "Now you know who the president's right-hand man is," with instructions to contribute money to his campaign. Nobody contributed to Rudolph Giuliani's gubernatorial campaign because in the end, he didn't run for governor. So, if you're wondering what the real problem with President Obama and me was, it was as such.

On June 7, 2008, after the last Democratic primary in Puerto Rico, Senator Hillary Clinton planned a press conference to announce her withdrawal from the presidential race and her support for Barack Obama. For some reason that even the physicist Niels Bohr and Albert Einstein probably wouldn't have been able to figure out, his campaign wanted the black congressional members to get up and endorse his presidential candidacy on June 6, the day before Senator Clinton would step down. My office was informed on the Wednesday preceding this Friday press conference, that I should be its moderator. I informed the Obama campaign that I'd supported Hillary Clinton, I'd be more than happy to support president Obama but would allow my candidate to get out of the race before my endorsement.

Our office received, what could only be described as a threat from the Obama campaign, whereupon I informed them that if Senator Obama did not call me before the press conference that I would make a statement after the press conference that I don't think they would appreciate very much.

So, at 1:30 on Friday June 7, two and a half hours prior to the press conference, Senator Obama called me and said, rather indignantly, "Hey listen, I told my people to leave you alone, it's New York, it's your state, it's your politics, you do whatever you want to do." I replied, "Senator, you are going to win the state of New York, it's a blue state, it's not contested. But one of the problems that you do have is a great deal of the money raised in presidential races comes from New York; 40 percent comes from two zip codes 10128, 10021 on the upper east side of Manhattan. I would like to make you aware of the fact that, had Hillary Clinton won the Democratic primary, that a lot of African Americans, maybe including even me—though I supported her—would feel, that once again, there is more inequality due to race than we'd like to admit, even in our own party. So, I'm sure you understand, Senator, that women are feeling right now, that the old-boys network beat racism, that Hillary Clinton pretty much had this election sewed up until your intervention, and that, white men would feel more comfortable with you than even a white woman."

He agreed with my assumption and I went on, "Either way, in New York, somebody has to go and tell the losing parties, women or African Americans, who, for the first time thought there was a chance that they would see one of their own as President, that we have to stick together as Democrats and that Senator McCain's plans for our country would not provide the environment that we need and that we need to stick together, and senator, who do you think would be the person that is going to have to have these conversations?"

"That would be you, governor, and I really hadn't thought about that part of it."

I was so angered by the treatment of Hillary by the Obama campaign, as in sore winners, that dragging the black congressional members—and only the black congressional members—out to make this endorsement, and the disrespect for me and my office, that it all came to fruition when I made this controversial remark: "Senator, I don't think you're thinking about a lot of things."

The vindictiveness that continued for the rest of the time that I was in office, was really the catalyst that the press conference was held in the first place. He seemed to think that all of these individuals would have abandoned a US senator from their own party to support his candidacy. One wonders if, in his old state Senate days, he would have gone against a leader of the Illinois party if a black candidate ran against them for national office. You can be assured that wouldn't have happened.

Accordingly, I received a second invitation to leave the campaign from a former supporter, who was speaking on behalf of Andrew Cuomo, in November 2009. While I did not back down a second time, I could understand why the attorney general would take advantage of this opportunity to run for governor because he was receiving White House support and anybody who had to shut down a budget deficit of over $20 billion would have easily offended a lot of people and would have exposed vulnerabilities.

A year prior, when I learned of the massive deficit confronting New York, I considered that no governor mired in such a predicament could survive an election having meted out the level of cuts and taxation to balance the budget. Had I announced that I would not seek my party's nomination, it would have nullified attack-ads from the special interests and threats from potential donors to my campaign. "This is a mess, and someone has to clean it up" I would say, announcing that I would not seek election in 2010. However, after some consultations, I decided to push on, believing that New Yorkers would inevitably understand that I took the necessary measures to prevent the state from becoming insolvent. The last state to default was Arkansas in 1929, and when it did the consequences were dire. When a state defaults, it can't pay its debts, it creates a run on the banks, and it brings commercial activity to a halt. This gives rise to high unemployment and an unfavorable credit rating. Basically everything falls apart.

In December of 2009, my campaign made an out-of-the-box move that had stunning results. We put campaign commercials on television in which I own up to mistakes that I'd made as Governor and talk about victories by raising the welfare allowance for the first time in twenty years thereby closing a budget gap, cleaning up New York's brownfields, and recognizing same-sex marriages from out of state, giving them full marital rights in New York. My poll numbers shot up to 43 percent and I was thinking that if I could move those poll numbers up 7 more points to 50, the attorney general would think twice about running for governor.

Obama's treatment of me and apparent opposition to me was made clearer in early October 2010 when Bill Clinton called me and asked me to meet with him at the Sheraton in New York that afternoon. I was very interested to hear what the President had to share with me, and it was this:

"Governor," said President Clinton, "I thought you might be wondering why President Obama seems to have a set against you and I have some thoughts on that I'd like to share."

"Yes, I had been wondering how I may have got the president off-side."

"Well, I believe Obama is pissed because you stood up for the Clintons."

"Really? And would you be willing to make your remarks public, Mr. President?"

"Well, Governor, you know that presidents do not criticize sitting presidents."

"Perhaps someone else could make a public statement?"

"No, that wouldn't work either."

"Well, in that case, Mr. President, I guess I just don't understand why we're having this conversation."

"Honestly, there isn't anything we can do about this, Governor, but I thought the least I could do was to thank you and share my thoughts. The best I can offer you is a hug."

The president then embraced me right there in his suite at the New York Sheraton and all I could say was "Oh my God! I have been accused of just about everything but now I'm going to be accused of having an affair with Bill Clinton."

And that, as they say, was that. Before we go on though, I just wanted to mention, that during my term of service we eradicated the Rockefeller drug laws which had the highest penalties for drug use and low-level drug dealing in the country. Also, I appropriated $600 million for stem cell research. My term certainly had its ups and downs, but all in all, I was, and remain, very satisfied with my gubernatorial service term. Had I not been stone-walled by Obama, Cuomo, and about fifty other people, I may have even have had a crack at the presidency. Or, better still, the vice presidency and another hooker incident. Although, these scandals don't seem to matter to people these days.

As for my successor, the 2020 COVID-19 pandemic revealed his true leader prowess and set him on a favored trajectory should he seek the White House in 2024. Commencing on March 16th, the Governor's organized, factual update, framed the policies that would best combat the pandemic. While issuing stern warnings against crowd density and insufficient federal support, he provided solace and compassion for Americans stricken by the sudden outbreak. "Who needs Dr. Phil?" I quipped in an interview with The Atlantic. "They should put Andrew on at 3:00 PM everyday to heal the American spirit. And so they did.

When President Trump admonished the states to finance the purchase of ventilators, the Governor thoroughly averred that competition between the individual states would drive the price of commodities sky high. When the President pronounced himself as the ultimate authority to reopen the government, a detailed exposition of the 10th amendment to the constitution, in response, silenced any further ravings on the part of the Chief Executive. For weeks, Governor Cuomo became the orator of responsibility for New Yorkers, as a weary nation listened and was soothed.

I harken back to 2002, when Andrew became an upstart candidate against New York Comptroller, H Karl McCall, for the opportunity to challenge New York's sitting Governor, George Pataki.

"Hey David," he urged me in a January phone call. "Are we going to let these old guys continue to run everything?"

"Andrew," I responded, "Are you suggesting that New York should be run by two Cuomos before we elect one African American?" We laughed. The best that can be said of any public servant is that they are willing to learn and grow, and we are seeing this right before our eyes in the most difficult of times.

12

What Do You Mean I'm Not Governor?

Sunday, January 24, 2010:

The Transport Worker's Union head, John Samuelson, was watching the American Football Conference championship game between the Indianapolis Colts and the New York Jets with some union members at a bar on the upper east side of Manhattan. The Jets were doing well until the second half. As was I. In the middle of the third quarter my press secretary contacts me to say that there's a report that I was making out with a woman in the executive mansion, in a closet. Whereupon, we were discovered by a state trooper doing security sweep in the mansion. The trooper gave the story to the *New York Post* reporter, Fred Dicker, and said he thought he'd be fired if it was discovered that he had done this. The trooper should have been fired for having hallucinations because there were no security sweeps being conducted by the state police in the executive mansion. The executive mansion is the governor's living quarters and only the state workers who were staff came into the building and that only happened from early morning to late at night. So if I had happened to be making out with a woman in the executive mansion, the last thing I would have been worried about was any troopers, so why would we be hiding in a closet? The story was totally bogus and was totally discounted by not only me but the state police and the governor's detail themselves.

A week prior I was having lunch with a family friend at The River Palm Restaurant on the other side of the George Washington Bridge in New Jersey. The lunch was originally scheduled for Patsy's on 117th Street and 1st Avenue in East Harlem, but was moved because the couple I knew, went to their daughter's soccer game in New Jersey. Later that evening my press secretary called to inform me that I was seen making out with this woman in a restaurant. This would be the first time there was a liaison between a man and a woman, where the woman was driven to the restaurant by her husband, who later on, came and picked her up. The witnesses to this incident actually didn't see it but were told about it by an individual who, later on, turned out the be a reporter. A second reporter heard the witnesses tell him this when they thought he was just a guy coming in to have a drink but they were not telling him what they actually saw but rather repeated what they were told by the first visitor. One of them said that when she looked at me when I was coming out of the men's room, 70 feet away, that I noticed she was looking at me and I had a guilty look. From 70 feet away. I wouldn't have noticed anybody. You know, because I'm blind. Everybody seems to keep forgetting.

Other patrons of the restaurant, when they read the news stories, took it upon themselves to contact the media and stated no such meeting ever happened. The media declined the invitation to look at the security footage offered by the restaurant that demonstrated that this was more made up nonsense.

Two weeks after the Jets played the Colts, the Colts appeared in the Super Bowl to take on the New Orleans Saints. At the kickoff, three news outlets were contacted simultaneously by individuals claiming that Governor David Paterson had been caught in a sex scandal that would generate more controversy than the Spitzer incident of two years prior. By halftime, the chyron on the TV screens were reporting that Governor Paterson will resign the following morning, February 8, 2010. I called my press secretary to inform him of this occurrence and he said, "We'll get on the phone and let the media know that this story is not true." I thought a minute, and then said to him, "You know something, I think we should let them report the story." He was quite shocked at the response. I said, "Yeah, let them report the story, build up a whole worldwide audience to see the governor of New York resign and tomorrow morning, I will not resign and I will respond to these rumors and innuendos myself."

Somehow between the time that I had this thought and an hour or two later, I was persuaded to let the media go ahead and push back on the story. This is when I think I knew, as Howard Cosell once said to Muhammad Ali, "you're not the man you were a couple of years ago." My plan was to let the story circulate. It would have been as worldwide as the Spitzer quagmire, and then walk into the press conference and say this, "Good morning, I know you are all here to cover the resignation of the governor but I'd like you to know that you've reached the wrong office. What you should be doing is looking up and researching your own sources because you're the one who knows who's perpetrating the lies, the distortions, and the innuendos that brought you here today. So since I know you'll be so busy, I'm going to go back to work. I'm not taking any questions and that you can get out of here and you can find out who is behind these vicious, vile rumors."

This could have given me a chance to speak to the world for myself and to address the fact that this was an organized, politically motivated attempt to accelerate my demise. Instead, the media reported, "although there would be no press conference on Monday morning, the governor's resignation is expected later in the week." This kept the farce going for a few more days. This mistake I made, this poor judgment in this situation was worse than the errors in the Senate appointment fiasco.

Earlier in the day of the Super Bowl, I got a call from Sherry Booker, she was the significant other, at one point, to my staff member, David Johnson. She told me that a *New York Times* reporter, David Kocieniewski, had come to her home and her twelve-year-old son answered the door. Mr. Kocieniewski asked for Ms. Booker. When told that she wasn't there, he went into the home with her minor child and called her from her son's cell phone. According to Ms. Booker, Kocieniewski said to her, "You won't believe the nasty things that Governor Paterson said about you." She inquired as to how he happened to be calling from her son's cell phone and when she found out that he was in the house, she ordered him to leave the home. But the reporters stayed outside waiting for her to return. Instead, she sent someone else to get the son, and took refuge somewhere in New Jersey, if memory serves me correctly. She asked me to get the media out from in front of her house whereupon I responded, "Sherry, if I can't get the media from out front of my house, what makes you think I can get them away from in front of yours?" She then asked why they were there in the first place. I told her that rumors were circulating around Albany, that she and some of her girlfriends had come to the executive mansion and had a drug and sex party with myself and David Johnson.

"Governor, I was in the audience of an event that you attended about two years ago and said hello, other than that I haven't seen you in three years."

"Sherry, that's just the way of the media, and right now, we'll just have to endure it."

I later learned that David Johnson himself had contacted the *Times* about reporters being in front of Ms. Booker's house the day before.

The day after, Monday, February 8th, the scheduled resignation time according to the media, I had a meeting with the editorial board of the *New York Times*. At one point I said to them that their reporters were harassing this woman. I named her and admonished them that one of the reporters went into the home of this woman whose child was persuaded to answer and open the door. I was informed by the chair of the *New York Times* Editorial Board, Eleanor Randolph, to refer this to the news department.

The following day, February 9th, a blog appeared confirming that these rumors were swirling around about this alleged wild party at the mansion. During the conversation with Sherry Booker, she alerted me that David Johnson was a danger to the staff, that he was going to be a real problem for me, and that she had real problems with him but didn't go into a great deal of detail about her beliefs. I knew the relationship between the two parties seemed to have come to an end about a year before and that Mr. Johnson, was now otherwise involved. Apparently, Mr. Johnson was paying for the apartment in which Ms. Booker was living, and they had a serious argument sometime in the fall. Johnson had advised me that she was very angry with him and might take some action against him. But he later told me that a mutual friend of theirs had advised him that she wasn't going to take any action against him but did not want to have any association with him.

Within two weeks, the Times wrote a story asserting that I had called Ms. Booker and asked her not to execute an order of protection against Mr. Johnson. Even if an elected official was going to talk to a staff member's significant other, you would think that a request would be not to press charges against him, but orders of protection are preventative and if you ever said something to someone like that, you're now taking responsibility for any action the other person would take thereafter and the violation of the order of protection might just be that they run into each other on the street but now you're on the hook because you asked the person not to bring the action in the first place. So the logic of anybody doing anything like this falls apart and eventually, so did the case because the day Sherry Booker called me, she wasn't sure if I was going to make some outlandish request on behalf of Mr. Johnson, so she had a friend of hers, who was a court stenographer, transcribe the entire conversation, which completely exonerated me.

Five months later Ms. Booker did press charges against Mr. Johnson, who pleaded to a violation and admitted to pushing her in an incident the prior fall. She testified and both her lawyers stated that I never asked her to do anything about the Johnson case because I didn't even know there was an issue about an order of protection in the first place. And yet, even today, you often read stories regarding Governor Paterson that *He was accused of interfering in a domestic violence situation involving a staff member.*

When this was originally written, many elected officials like Congressmember Nita Lowey and even the newly-minted senator Kirsten Gillibrand, said that "If this turns out to be right, the governor must resign." This would be the first time there was ever an accusation but no accuser. The lawyers said Ms. Booker never made the accusations. Ms. Booker testified and said that she never made the accusations, and the witness who transcribed the tapes said that there was no accusation and also documented it.

A week later, the *Daily News* printed a story accusing me of going to Florida on campaign money but actually using the time for vacation. We immediately produced the dates and times of the people that I saw and that accusation was quashed.

Next up was the public integrity commission of New York State that charged me with accepting six free tickets to the World Series opening game between the Yankees and the Phillies in 2009. The public integrity commission's report does not include a letter from my counsel, Peter Kiernan, only requesting a ticket for the Governor. Therefore we had the full intent of paying for the other five tickets. When asked why the public integrity commission never included that letter in their report, their response was "Who was the attorney speaking for when he wrote the letter?" The person who wanted the tickets, which was me. The commission also made a perjury referral to the district attorney's office when I answered that I fully intended to pay for the other tickets and would pay whatever fine was necessary if they ruled that I wasn't allowed to accept the ticket on my own. I took the position because three governor's counsels, and one counsel to Governor Pataki, had all advised that if the activity takes place in the state for which the governor serves, and the majority of the people in the audience are constituents of the governor, that the governor could accept an invitation, particularly to notable events such as the first game of the World Series, or, in Governor Spitzer's case, the first winter classic, an outdoor hockey game played between the New York Rangers and the home team, Buffalo Sabers.

The public integrity commission decided that I wasn't telling the truth and fined me $96,000 originally. The case was appealed to an administrative law judge who ruled that there were two violations on my part, one inadvertent and one undetermined whether it was deliberate or not and fined me $5000 for each offense making it $10,000. The public integrity commission changed the amount of the fine to $62,000, which I paid in February of 2011, as soon as the decision was rendered. Now, an individual, who has become president, has invented the phrase fake news, but I ask you, Mr. Trump, what would you call this? Fake news to the power of ten? A deliberate staging of dramatic and shocking events, all of which were false, to impugn the character of a governor who had angered many special interest groups because he wanted to keep the state from becoming insolvent.

On February 26, 2010, I stood before a press conference and announced that I would not be a candidate for Governor of the state of New York in the year 2010. Beleaguered and shocked by the events in the last few months, knowing that eight weeks before I was regaining support that I had lost over the budget battles and some misadventures with particular appointments. I would never have dreamed that I would live fifty-five and a half years without being accused of anything, and then, within a space of fifty days, accused of everything short of being a gunman in the St. Valentine's Day massacre of 1929. But as they say in the infomercials, "But wait, there's more!"

Now, the media's misreporting that I'm about to resign from office. I had informed them repeatedly that I was not resigning because I didn't do anything wrong and that we could get together a year from now and we would find that not one of these allegations had been proven. That turned out to be right, but nonetheless, the media continued this pursuit of bringing down a second New York governor, to the point that they announced that it would occur over the weekend of March 5th, 2010.

On Saturday the 6th, Larry Schwartz, the new secretary to the governor, informed me that he had not gotten a response from phone calls made to the Lieutenant Governor, Richard Ravitch, who seemed to have disappeared for the last thirty-six hours. He also said that he had credible evidence that Ravitch had gone to meet with Attorney General Andrew Cuomo about the imminent transfer of power in the state. When I was lieutenant governor, knowing that the governor was in imminent danger for approximately two and a half days, at all points I tried to avoid any inference that would be drawn, that I was contributing to the problem. When we finally caught up with Ravitch he told us some story about how the Attorney General has summoned him to his office to talk about the transference of power and he accused Attorney General Cuomo of requesting that, if he, Ravitch, became governor, that he not appoint an African American as lieutenant governor to finish out his term. A very bizarre conclusion to a very unbelievable situation. Ravitch has gone on over the years to document and write articles and give interviews about why the members of my staff never listened to him. He did not accuse me of this but said they were unresponsive to him. After a performance like this, what other reaction would he expect? Knowing that I was dead set against the delaying of any debt that needed to be paid by the state and had already closed a $21 billion deficit in 2009, I was not endeared to a Rockefeller Institute proposal that he promoted in which the state would borrow $6 billion and pay it back over three years to provide services during this economic crisis. In addition, the Governor would be granted special powers during the crisis to address the issue without support from the legislature. This proposal, known as—strangely enough—the Ravitch plan, was DOA because we were opposed to any borrowing in such a circumstance. In addition, these special powers would be granted approximately every thirty years—when you have a monumental economic crisis—whereas the powers that the legislature would get while participating in the submission of the budget, would happen every year and would guarantee it would be late every year, but its submission would be similarly delinquent.

I was riding on the state plane with my longtime associate, now my assistant, Howie Katz, when turbulence shook the plane violently in a fashion I had not experienced in all my travels on the state helicopters and planes. Howie looked quite perturbed by the circumstances, whereupon I grabbed his arm and said,

"Don't you know what this is?"

"What is it?"

"It's the Ravitch plan."

Of course, I myself, appointed Richard Ravitch to be my lieutenant governor. Even over the objections of Attorney General Andrew Cuomo, Dean Skelos, and Pedro Espada now sharing the leadership of the state Senate Republican party, which, at that time, was in the majority. As stated earlier, I appointed Ravitch because I wanted a civic leader and not anyone with any political ties, so that the lawsuit that I was expecting, would be guided by the legal question of whether a governor had the power to appoint a lieutenant governor, rather than who the lieutenant governor might be. When the Republicans sued, Senator Skelos pointed out he didn't have any problem with the qualifications of Mr. Ravitch other than the fact that the governor had no constitutional authority to appoint him. The other abject objector was Donald John Trump.

July 14, 2009:

I received a letter from Donald Trump. Now please be advised that if you ever get a letter from Donald Trump, you're not going to find it in your mailbox. You're going to discover it on television. I never actually received the hard copy of the letter, but I did see a tape of an appearance he made on CNBC to announce that, in his words, "The governor was doing such a good job but why would he appoint a person to succeed him who was incompetent and incapable of running government or conducting any other type of business?"

As this was the only objection to my selection of Lieutenant governor, I was bemused and summoned Ravitch for a tete-a-tete to discuss the issue. "I have made my decision and this letter has no bearing on it, Dick," I said to him when we met. "But I'm just curious as to why your selection would ignite such a volatile reaction from Mr. Trump." Ravitch had his own story to tell and it had to do with the construction of the Hyatt Hotel at 42nd and Lexington. Thirty-one years ago, which would have placed it at approximately 1978, built a new subway entrance at that location. Ravitch ran the MTA as a member of the Carey administration. Ravitch received a phone call from Trump asking that a side entrance from the station, into the building where his employees worked, might be erected during the construction. Ravitch expressed that there was no problem with the idea and would assess how much Mr. Trump had to pay for the additional effort. "Are you kidding!?" Trump said, according to Ravitch. "I do so many things for the city that you should build this entrance for free, and if you don't agree to do this, I'm going straight to the governor!" Well, apparently Ravitch did not concede to his request. Neither did the governor. And the station entrance was built without a side entrance. Trump was apparently still angry about it thirty years later.

So, life goes on until eight months later, when Ravitch, as Lieutenant Governor, was publicizing his plan to borrow $6 billion dollars over a period of three years to soften the budget-cutting measures that had been issued by me in my formal budget presentation to the legislature in January. His theory was to offer this olive branch to the legislature, along with the promise of participation in the actual budget planning process, in exchange for added supervisory powers that would be awarded to the governor in periods of economic crisis. As this differed with my actions over the last two budgets, in which I urged that we could no longer kick the can down the road and had to engage in a disciplined reduction of services, the media was quite interested in how Ravitch viewed the budget process as it stood. And so, they asked him when he came out of a meeting in March 2010. His general response was that the governor's budget was "pretty good," but he wasn't sure the legislature would pass it, and this promoted him to front page coverage involving this issue.

Not endeared at all to these remarks, I was sitting in my office dismayed over this entire episode when my secretary, Narda Singh, announced to me in a joyous way, that I have a phone call from Donald Trump. It never occurred to me that it had anything to do with what was causing my apprehension. Halfway between my saying Hello Donald, I was overwhelmed with a cacophony of cross outbursts including something like "Hey David, I warned you and look at this! The guy is an asshole, he is untrustworthy, and he is disloyal. I told you, you shouldn't have taken this guy and you should have listened to me." Pausing to establish my equilibrium, I said, "Donald, today is the day when I just don't have the strength to argue with you but it's always wonderful to hear from you and thank you for thinking of me." So, Donald had had his moment and I was back at work fifteen minutes later when both of my office doors fly open at the same time and I am confronted with a chorus of rebukes as in,

"Governor, why did you tell the associated press that you wish you'd never taken Ravitch in the first place?"

"I did not make those remarks" I retorted.

"Well, Donald Trump just told the AP that he talked to you just a few minutes ago and that's what you said."

Whereupon I emptied the office and summoned Narda to retrieve Mr. Trump for a second conversation.

"Donald, first of all, I didn't know you were working for Candid Camera"—an old CBS TV comedy show where people were filmed without their knowledge—"and secondly, I never said that I'm sorry that I took Ravitch. I think it was clear to you that I'm angry with Ravitch but it's the first time he's ever made a mistake like this so I'm going to just talk to him about it and warn him about the ramifications if he does it again. So please tell me why you told the Associated Press that I did say it" and thereupon, I was engaged in a response that I would become all too familiar with over the coming years.

"But it's the truth, it's the truth! You do wish you hadn't taken him. Look me in the eye and tell me that isn't the truth."

"I can't look you in the eye, we're on the telephone."

Not a word.

"I extend to you a courtesy that you did not extend to me, I will be going on the media in the next fifteen minutes to assure them that I did not make this statement about Mr. Ravitch, which is the truth."

"Oh David, come on! You're not going to take me on over an issue like this one, are you?"

As promised a statement was released from my press office within the half hour that I did not make that statements as said by Donald Trump. But that wasn't the end of the story.

Donald showed up on the Sean Hannity show within the week in response to the question, that had nothing to do with state politics, and roared that the biggest problem with New York was its Governor who is incompetent and too paralyzed by fear to manage the affairs of the state. The next time we would meet was on July 4, 2013, when I was a guest at his Golf Club in Westchester. I was in line to get food when someone shouted out, "Hey David, ya wanna hamburger?" It was Donald behind the grill, and he made me a hamburger and handed it to me and I said to him, "Do I need a taster?" and we both laughed.

On December 30, 2014, we met again at Mar-a-Lago where I was sitting at a table with my longtime friend, Jeff Greene, his wife Mei Sze, and five other guests. The future president swooped in to inquire as to what area I'm working these days and then invited me to a New Year's party planned for the following evening. I was trying to get a gauge about how the other guests at the table felt about the invitation, but no one is talking. So I said, "well, we've got a lot of things to do tomorrow night." "Come on, David, you don't have to stay all night, you can come for a little while, Rod Stewart will be here." Well, that was certainly enough for me and I decided, "we'll drop by for a little while."

When Donald sauntered off to another table, my friend pointed out that I had just made $3200 for Donald Trump, which surprised me. My curiosity was assuaged when Jeff reminded me that he was a member of Mar-a-Lago and that each guest that came to the New Year's Eve party with him would generate a charge of $400 per person. "The last time I checked," Jeff said, "8 x $400 is $3200. Tell Donald you should get a commission for that."

Oddly enough on the afternoon of December 31, the next day, while having lunch at Mar-a-Lago, Donald came and sat with me and we eventually covered the incident of seven years prior.

"You know, Governor, I probably wouldn't have said what I did that day but I was completely frustrated that this Ravitch guy, who knew what your position had been and the accolades you received for tackling the difficult budget of 2008–2009 at that time, and that he wanted to borrow $6 billion and give it to the legislature to prolong the fact that they were continuingly refusing to cut the budget and I thought was completely out of line for his position."

I was absolutely stunned, because Trump was not aware that his sentiments mirrored those of my top staff members, who couldn't believe that Ravitch was acting this way. When one of them tried to admonish him, he later told me that he said to Ravitch, "Come on we all work for the governor," and Ravitch's response was "No, I work 'with' the governor." Ravitch has gone on to generate about ten articles since we left office about why nobody was listening to him, when in fact, we listened to him but didn't agree with him.

There was even a quote from Paul Volcker, the former head of the Federal reserve, wondering why nobody listened to the lieutenant governor. This despite that the "Ravitch Plan," as he called it, would have curtailed the powers of the Governor even further than for governors in most states. It would have overturned the results of the case Silver v Pataki, as well as a public referendum in 2006 that rejected this claim that the legislature should share in the production of the budget in addition to the passing of the document, when the budget had been late in meeting its deadline of April 1, during twenty-two of the last twenty-five years. It's now possible that the budget wouldn't have even been issued until April 1 if the three parties conferred before its introduction. Thus, Ravitch, as Andrew Cuomo, the attorney general—and inevitable governor—warned me, was doing the bidding of the legislative leaders, and his rotund frame, the only thing I know of that is larger than his ego, was noticed in several of their offices while I was trying to pass the budget.

As these articles trickled out in various newspapers after I left office, Shaun Darcy, former press secretary to governors Corzine, Codey, and McGreevey in New Jersey, now working with me, kept saying to me,

"Hey Gov, when are we gonna get this guy?"

"Well Shaun, we just did."

I ATTENDED A church service at Cornerstone Baptist Church in Brooklyn, at the invitation of Congressman Hakeem Jeffries. At a point in the service, after I spoke, all of the elders came up and prayed, each of them placing their hands on my head, shoulders, and back. The evening prior, I was so badgered and fearful of the press that when I came home to an empty apartment, as my family was spending a weekend in Albany, I was afraid to put the lights on because I knew they were watching my apartment. I put a plate in the microwave and then actually ate my dinner on the shelf of the refrigerator, where I could see, leaving the refrigerator door open until I was finished. At this point, I had an out-of-body experience. I watched myself cowering under the pressure of this relentless harassment. I scraped my plate, closed the refrigerator, turned on every light in my apartment, walked out onto the terrace and waved hello to the media. During this church service, I felt the same resilience, feeling so blessed as a result of the actions of the minister and the elders. When I walked out of the church, of course, the media was there to greet me and said, "Did you pray for yourself?" I said, "No, I prayed for you."

Feeling complaisant, *but complacent,* as a result of the last couple of months, I managed to re-engage with the legislature and work on my last budget, 2010–2011. The legislature would just not close the budget and even good government people, like state senator Liz Dunning Krueger, called me up and said, "Well, we got to within $2.5 billion, isn't that enough?"

As well-meaning as the request was, it wasn't enough. The budget has to be balanced, constitutionally. Unlike the previous two years, the legislature passed extenders, which is the same thing that Congress does when the government is going to shut down if there's no budget. Angry that they weren't addressing the issue, my budget director, Robert Megna, adroitly offered them a proposal that had no perks and no fluffs, and he said, "we're cutting things down to the bone." But I misunderstood him and in a radio interview with Susan Arbetter of PBS, I assured the public, don't worry we're already getting cuts even though the budget isn't passed. Megna, along with Larry Schwartz, my secretary, and Peter Kiernan, my counsel, descended on me to alert me to the fact that we weren't cutting the budget, we just weren't giving the legislature a few perks to try to ensure cooperation and eventual passage. "So why can't we cut the budget in the extenders," I asked. Whereupon Larry Schwartz and Peter Kiernan let me know that they had actually considered this themselves and Peter Kiernan was having the matter researched. The final conclusion that was given to us in the next couple of days, was that the difference between the budget process and the extenders is that the Governor writes the extenders, the legislature has to vote it up or down, there are no amendments, no changes, no rejections, or overriding the governor's veto. It's either take it or leave it. We called it the nuclear option and we exercised it. We then put our cuts in the next week's budget extender and the legislature either had to vote it into effect or shut down the government.

Speaker Sheldon Silver and I had a very good relationship and it was often kind of a father-and-son relationship because he had sixteen years of doing the budget as the speaker and gave me a lot of valuable information, but he would always sort of find a way to make me feel guilty, even accusing my staff members of scheduling meetings on the Jewish holidays in October when half of them were Jewish. This was just sort of his way of getting the advantage because I would have been very hurt if I found out my staff was disrespecting the holiest of holidays. So, when I presented the nuclear option to Speaker Silver and the new majority leader John Sampson, I knew that it was not going to be embraced but I was really amazed at how angry the speaker became. He then quoted the names of all the governors he'd served under and said he never saw a more naked political power-grab than he had just observed. I cautioned him that I could think of one that's worse.

He responded, "Please tell me what that is."

"What I'm going to do tomorrow, Shelly," I replied.

One of the causes of the budgetary problems were the legislator's discretionary member items which I informed them they would not receive until they balanced the budget. Instead, they piled them all up, issuing them individually so they couldn't be vetoed as a whole. This amounted to 6,709 individual requests for funding to different community-based organizations. Before I could read one of them, he had a press conference suggesting I wouldn't read any of them and I wouldn't even know what they meant and I would use the Governor's auto pen, which goes through and vetoes them separately. I came up with an idea to demonstrate that I wasn't going to ignore their requests. I had them piled up on a table that must have consisted of two two-and-a-half-foot-high piles of bills. I then had them passed by a staff member to my counsel, read the premise of the bill, passed it to me, where I vetoed it and passed it to another member who stamped it, who then passed it to another member who filed it. After an hour of this torture, we took a break, whereupon my press secretary, Morgan Hook, brilliantly came up with the idea of filming the entire process. For eight and a half hours, New Yorkers could watch the governor single-handedly veto, with his own pen, 6,709 bills. The *New York Times*, the *Daily News*—sounding like a Billy Joel song—and the *New York Post* made this a front page story and the bill signing episode, well, it became a legend. I started signing David A. Paterson, then it became David Paterson, then D. Paterson, then D.A.P., then D.P. and then one stroke which was kind of a D and a P connected. I don't think I've ever signed my name correctly since.

In the summer of 2010, as LeBron James was taking his talents to play for the Miami Heat, we completed the budget process late, but with a new power devised by our efforts which would enable Governor Andrew Cuomo to pass every budget in his first two terms on time. Different research groups, including the Rockefeller Institute, rated the powers of New York's governor in the bottom quintile of the country's states. This one edit moved New York's gubernatorial powers into the top half. Interacting with Attorney General Cuomo, as he pursued the nomination, and then successfully won as New York's 56th governor, I learned that his administrative capabilities were nonpareil and his evaluation techniques of different circumstances were equally extraordinary.

For instance, back in March 2010, when lieutenant governor Ravitch wanted to institute the "Ravitch Plan," which would basically reverse a famous supreme court case, Silver v. Pataki, in which the legislative challenged the powers of the governor in court and the governor won. Then, there was a public referendum which the governor also won to keep the powers as strong as they were. Speaking with me on the phone that day, Andrew Cuomo—then attorney general—asked me this question. "Can you please explain the Silver v. Pataki case?" I felt very defensive about being asked this question but managed to choke out about a paragraph of somewhat obtuse concepts. Cuomo paused a minute and said, "You know, I would think if you were to ask me the question, your answer was about where I would be." Meaning neither one of us knows very much about this case. I agreed, so Andrew then said to me, "well, probably the only two people who really know anything about this case are former Governor Pataki and Speaker Silver, and I would suggest a couple of counsels know about it and no one else. Again, I agreed. Then Cuomo said, "So which one of them do you think is speaking to Dick Ravitch?" And it hit me like a ton of bricks, who it was.

So this ability to really dispassionately look at different situations, and the conduct of others, and to fathom what the motives behind all of it is, has really served the Governor well in his two terms.

Meanwhile, there was an incident involving a Chinese gentleman who was an immigrant to this country by the name of King Woo. King Woo had gotten into some trouble as a teenager and had been sent to a youthful offender facility. When he got out he went ahead and completed high school and college, did graduate work, and became a leader in Chinatown. There was a desire to appoint him to some sort of committee, either by the borough president, or one of the city council members, whereupon he was advised to apply for citizenship, as he was an immigrant from China when he was four or five years old. He did not speak the Chinese language as his family left at such a young age. When ICE realized Mr. Woo had been convicted of a crime, even though it was seventeen years previous, they took him into custody and held him in the sixth circuit in some facility in Texas. He was scheduled for deportation until that process was interrupted by a pardon issued by the governor of the state of New York and now without the underlying crime, the deportation was prevented, and Mr. Woo returned to his family and his work in New York City.

Peter Kiernan and I decided to set up an immigration pardon panel where we would pardon immigrants who had committed minor offenses and were being deported for seemingly reckless and inhuman reasons. We pardoned a gentleman from Long Island who shot and killed an intruder into his home. He was not charged by the district attorney but was recommended for deportation. The Immigration and Naturalization Service considered the conviction for maintaining an unlicensed weapon was the reason for the deportation, but once again the pardon intervened. A woman who hailed from Peru and left the country when she was sixteen years old, passed a bad check when she was nineteen, and was convicted of a misdemeanor. Thirty-seven years later, at the age of fifty-six, there was an attempt to deport her which was also stopped. A woman from Nigeria was also going to be deported for the same reason, but she had a six-year-old autistic child who would be left without any family connection and therefore we granted the pardon.

In all, there were thirty-nine immigrations pardons that were granted and to date, none of them have been repeat offenders. We also commuted the sentence of a man named John White who was a resident of Miller Place in Suffolk County, Long Island. The great author, Michael D'Antonio, who doesn't live far from Miller Place, said, "If you want to know what life was like in the South in the 1930s, visit Miller Place sometime." Mr. White's son was accused of some improper conduct with a sister of a white teenager at a party and was chased from the party by a mob. He drove home and went into his father's room and told his father that the mob is coming to the house to attack him. His father, John White, told his wife to call 911 and took a firearm outside where he confronted a mob of about twelve people standing on his lawn in a semicircle around him. One of the members, a young man of about seventeen, ran up and punched the gun, trying to unleash it from White's hand. White bobbled the gun but then fired it, killing the young man. White was not allowed to claim self-defense at his trial because there was no evidence that he was ever retreating. The defense countered that White could not have retreated because the perpetrators were on both sides of him and he didn't want to turn his back to any of them. Nonetheless, he was convicted of manslaughter and sentenced in spite of the indignation of the judge who reported that the law just didn't have a way for him to let Mr. White go without jail time. At the end of my term, I commuted the sentence of John White.

My wife and I attended a traditional dance given by an organization known as the Comas. The members and their guests, almost all of whom were black, were elated that I had commuted the sentence of this man who otherwise had no criminal record. One gentleman ran up and hugged me so tight I thought he was going to choke me and I said, "So, I surmise this is because you're happy with the decision involving John White?" He looked at me and said, "Governor, I *am* John White."

There was a panel that was set up internally—not by me—in the governor's office to review decisions that I'd made and voted four to one that I not commute the sentence of Mr. White. At a press conference a few days later when I was asked why didn't I listen to the panel, I asked the press, "Which one of those people sitting on the panel calls themselves Governor?" Ironically enough, both the *Daily News* and the *New York Post* wrote editorials in support of my pardoning John White, the *Post* adding, "if this were Texas, there wouldn't have even been a trial."

On July 16th, 2010, I signed a bill preventing the police—after stopping and frisking and taking information from citizens—from holding the information for future episodes. The contention of the bill was that if people are stopped and frisked and found to be doing nothing wrong, there's no reason that the law enforcement should be collecting records against them, assuming that we're still in the United States of America.

I signed the bill over the fierce objections of Police Commissioner Raymond Kelly and Mayor Michael Bloomberg, who advised me that there would be a number of lawsuits if I signed that bill. At the time of the release of this book, there hasn't been a single one. So, I hope you understand why I took the action, Mayor.

AS MENTIONED PREVIOUSLY, on September 25th, 2010, I appeared on *Saturday Night Live*. People have always appreciated my sense of humor but my sense of humor is just how I'm feeling. I've never actually tried to be funny and the thought of trying to do it on national television was overwhelming. I was coached by my daughter, Ashley, and we went to *Saturday Night Live* for a 6 o'clock walk-through and had a full dress rehearsal at 9 o'clock. Everything went swimmingly, but then, around 11 o'clock, half an hour before the live show would begin, Ashley asked me if I wanted to go to the room next door to where we were housed, to have a drink with Justin? Justin was Justin Timberlake, but now it's just "Justin." I declined that, within 5 minutes, the exhaustion of the previous 5 hours' work overwhelmed me, I couldn't remember any of my lines. No teacher was ever harder on me than Ashley as she kept badgering me to keep rehearsing. Charles O'Byrne, who was present that evening, put his hands on my shoulders and said, "Look, David, you're a funny guy, these are professional comedians. If you can't think of what to say, just say what comes natural and they will work with you." So I was pushed in a rolling chair, right up to the desk of Weekend Update, right next to Fred Armisen who was imitating me, and I put my hand on his shoulder and said, "Stop, stop, stop!" Suddenly, all of my lines came back. That episode of *Saturday Night Live* has been shown a number of times in repeat, and I must say, my friend Jeff Greene was right when he said, "David you fought the good fight, you stood up to the malicious way they treated the disabled, now go on the show and do your thing."

It's great to walk down the street and people walk up to you and they say, "Governor, thank you for your service," and they shake your hand. But there's nothing like when a bunch of kids start running across from the other side of the street and say, "Hey, you're the guy from *Saturday Night Live*."

By October of 2010, news of my immigration pardon panel had spread so wide that people had decided; whatever they did wrong, they could get a pardon for it. A former doctor of mine—he became former because I didn't grant his son a pardon for his conviction in a Medicare fraud case—wanted a pardon before the son was even sentenced for the crime.

Another man, speaking through his family member, wanted a pardon because he had beat up his girlfriend about fifteen years before and fled the jurisdiction. Now he was back and thought maybe he could get a pardon when he hadn't even been arrested for the crime yet.

Finally, there was a commutation request from Judith Alice Clark, who had participated in the Brinks holdup of 1981 in Rockland County. She was driving the getaway car. Two police officers and two Brinks security guards were shot in this robbery. One of the police officers survived but died twenty years later in one of the towers at the World Trade Center, after the attack on our country. In my career, I was always an opponent of the death penalty and our idea that the replacement for the death penalty would be life without parole. This was a life without parole case, therefore, I did not think it was proper or right to commute the sentence of someone, even though they had made extraordinary progress in their life and had really become a role model and leader for other inmates and an important personality. Even on the outside during her incarceration all kinds of people came forward to speak on behalf of Ms. Clark, including former borough president Ruth Messenger, former councilman Ronny Eldridge, former public advocate Mark Green, the list went on and on but I still feel that this was the right decision, because; had there been a death penalty—under the circumstances of the conviction—she would have been eligible and the sentence she received was tantamount to life without parole. Every year a candlelight vigil is held for the terrible tragedy that happened in 1981 and I wouldn't want any of the people attending to feel that I didn't acknowledge the grief of the families and the people of that neighborhood.

In November, Senator Charles Schumer was re-elected to the United States Senate, Senator Kirsten Gillibrand was elected to fill the end of the vacant term left by Hillary Clinton, Eric Schneiderman was elected as New York's Attorney General, and Thomas DiNapoli was elected as New York's comptroller for the first time—after being seated by the legislature in 2007 following the resignation of Alan Hevesi, who inevitably served time for corruption. Robert Duffy was elected Lieutenant Governor, running on the ticket with the new Governor of the State of New York, Andrew M. Cuomo.

I went to his inauguration on January 1, 2011 and heard him say, "Where would the state be without the intervention of Governor Paterson? This state had the greatest economic problems during that time of all the states but he helped weather the storm and steered us back into prosperity." Sitting in the audience, I heard those remarks and thought, *just to be alive and well and to hear that statement coming from the new Governor erased all the abuse and indignation I felt from the reaction to trying to do the right thing.*

Sometimes I think because I was not elected, that I felt a greater duty to be fair, to be honest, and to represent all the people of the state of New York.

So, as I walked out of the capital for the first day as a private citizen on January 1, 2011, and headed back to New York City, I felt a sense of enlightenment and wondered whether or not history would shine through a malaise of hostility and contempt for so many of my efforts. But I knew that I had done the best job that I could possibly offer.

If I could go back and do things differently I certainly would have done so.

If I could go back and try harder to do the right thing, I certainly could not have done so.

13

On the Radio

September 6, 2011:

This is a day I thought I'd never see. I'm actually going to have my own radio show on WOR 710 AM in New York City. My first guests were former United States Senator Alfonse D'Amato and former Mayor Ed Koch, who came on to congratulate me on the show. My first show also included a debate between Assemblyman David Weprin and businessman Bob Turner, who would be running in a special election to fill a congressional seat in the county of Queens.

Lacking the technology, equipment, and the venues to learn much as a child, I used the radio to fill the information gap caused by my blindness and lack of services. My teachers were the radio hosts Barry Gray, Long John Nebel, and Barry Farber. There was a great talk show on New York's black radio station, WWRL, hosted by Bernie McCain, and eventually by a man named Bob Law. I remember hearing an interview with the Duke of Windsor, conducted by a woman who used the moniker Martha Deane on WOR in the late 1960s. It wasn't until forty years later when I saw *The King's Speech* that I discovered what a bastard he really was, but in those days, everyone was romanticizing how he gave up his crown for the woman he loved.

My political awareness was enhanced by two talk show hosts who replaced a rock 'n' roll station on WMCA—Alex Bennett and Leon Lewis. Howard Cosell had one of the best talk shows I'd ever heard. It was broadcast every Sunday night and it was called *Speaking of Everything*. Otherwise, my favorite sportscaster was Bill Mazer, who basically started sports talk radio.

I was given the opportunity to substitute host by a talk show host named Jay Diamond on the old WEVD—formerly WHN in New York City. I'd had a couple of other opportunities to substitute host including for John Gambling on WOR, starting when I left office in early 2011, but now this was my show, a 4-6 PM drive-time program in the largest market in the country. Things did not go well because most of the audiences were fiercely conservative and did not take well to the suggestion there was an alternative view to theirs. But, as I started my second year, to my surprise, I started to move the needle, because most people thought that I was fair and that I did not always come down on what they considered to be the hopelessly liberal point of view about everything.

My favorite show was my interview with a person who believed he knew the exact identity of the zodiac killer, and by the end of the show he had convinced me, and most of the audience, of who it might be.

Tom Voight was a researcher and an advocate who attended many seminars surrounding the suspicious killings of individuals known to have been committed by the self-named Zodiac Killer in the California bay area during the late 1960s and into the 1970s. After one of his attacks, he notified the Vallejo police department that he was the killer, and the police officer who answered the phone later heard a voice which Voight played for her. She responded was that this was the same person who called her to report the shootings.

About fifteen years later, a former member of a black separatist group reported to police that a white person, who was the editor of their newspaper, might be the actual killer. The authorities dismissed this assertion, but Tom Voight and many advocates did not. There were a couple of men who underwent an intense amount of scrutiny involving the killings, but the entry of this possible suspect came almost twenty years later. There is some DNA evidence and with the recent apprehension of the Golden State Killer, over forty years later, it will be interesting to see if this process identifies perhaps the most well-known serial killers in the country. The Zodiac Killer used to leave coded messages for the police and one decoder believes that they broke the code, revealing the name of the aforementioned suspect. This interview was a thriller.

My least favorite show occurred on Friday, December 14, 2012.

A week later I would be fired, but I didn't know it then. Interestingly enough, I usually arrived in the studio around 2 o'clock to spend a good two hours preparing for my show. On this particular day, I was in the studio at noon to have conversations with Dick Traum, the founder of the Achilles Track Club, and the chairman of the board, Robert Katz. They wanted me to assume chairmanship of the board beginning in 2013, which I gladly accepted. In my conversation with Katz, I told him I had just heard a story that a couple of children had been killed in a grade school in Newtown, Connecticut, and both of us experienced the melancholy that accompanies such a tragedy. The noon-to-two host, Joan Hamburg, had a taped program on that day and when I remarked to Scott Lakefield, who was the program director at WOR, that I could tell by the slow processing of the information to the public that this was a much greater tragedy than they were saying right now. Scott asked me if I would consider going on the air early and I would preempt the noon to two show to report on this Newtown tragedy. So around 1:30, without any preparation, and with scant information, I went on the air accompanied by the late Dr. Joy Brown, who hosted an advice show on the station.

By now the police were reporting a significant death toll. There was also a report of a potential shooter, and his name was rippling through the media. At this point, it was the brother of the actual shooter, who was lambasted throughout social media for hours until the mistake was corrected. Finally, by two o'clock, officials confirmed twenty-six deaths—twenty of the victims being primary school age—as well as six teachers. Now I have had a long career of promoting restrictions on the use of firearms. However, I expressed my indignation at politicians who use any tragedy instantly to promote their views on government actions that should be taken to restrict guns. I feel our society has become jaded from our instant conversion from a human tragedy to a politicized opportunity within a half hour.

Fortunately, President Obama went on air about four o'clock and spoke about the tragedy in personal terms. He was visibly shaken by the incident and didn't address the ramifications for government and Congress as he would weeks later.

Six months earlier, I had talked to one of those present in a Colorado movie theater, when a man in full military gear walked to the front of the theater and started shooting at the audience, killing several people. This was an anxious moment for me, but the sadness and despair that I felt for five hours being on the air during that horrible tragedy in Connecticut was my most difficult radio host challenge.

ALTHOUGH I'D IMPROVED my ratings, when Clear Channel Communications bought WOR in December of 2012, I didn't think I was long for the station and went in and told them it was alright with me, but for some reason they went through the formality of dismissing me about two hours before what would have been my show on that day. Knowing that some Clear Channel executives were sitting in the conference room, I went in and opened the door, and of course, when someone is dismissed and they invade a board-room meeting, there is cause for concern, but before they could respond, I said "Wow, you guys are really tough, even when I was governor they let me stay to the end of the year."

In the spring of 2013, Jerry Crowley, who had been my benefactor and hired me to work at WOR, was now working at a station known as *The Answer* in Hackensack, New Jersey. When they were forced to fire one of their talk show hosts, Crowley didn't want a lot of backlash or publicity about this move and asked me if I would come in and co-host the show to distract the listeners from the change in hosting. The other host was the head of the Guardian Angels, Curtis Sliwa. Curtis hosted a famous number-one rated morning show on WABC years before. Contrary to *Point-Counterpoint* days of *Saturday Night Live*, Curtis and I had a show that was more based on humor and also historical references we shared since we were born within two months of each other.

NOVEMBER 5TH, 2013:

I went to a luncheon at Le Cirque restaurant in New York, which featured the Prince and Princess of Serbia to showcase their charity work for the disabled and displaced citizens of their country. After completing a photo session with many of the guests and speakers who were speaking at the event, a woman came up and said to me, "Governor, I hope you don't mind if I introduce myself, I'm Mary Sliwa." Immediately realizing this was the former wife of my radio partner, and that there was a high-profile child support battle that often reached the newspapers, I contemplated how to effect a brief hello and an immediate exit. Before I could make my hasty exit, Mary said to me that her son Anthony remembered me. Anthony at the time was aged 9 and was working around some speech and language difficulties and I found it hard to believe that Anthony would remember who I was, so I was very touched to hear that he mentioned my name at home.

Engrossed in the conversation with Mary, I found her to be truly elegant and very bright. There appeared to be polar, nay galactic differences between her and her former husband. I was baffled as to how these two people could have ever gotten together. She exuded such warmth that, at the end of the conversation, I told her how nice it was to speak with her and I hugged her; which I would never do in 99 percent of cases. Walking down the street after the event, I thought; why did I do that? I'll probably be in the next court papers. Although there *were* some next court papers, they didn't include me, but they were quite unflattering toward my former radio partner.

I encountered Mary again six days later at an event for the Eye Care Unit of Mount Sinai hospital, hosted at the Metropolitan Club and chaired by, my former wife, and me. By this time, Michelle and I were separated but still happy to host events together. Mary and I were among the first guests to arrive and this time we got the chance to talk for about forty-five minutes, at the end of which I was in full crush modality.

January 2014, Mary called me to thank me for giving Anthony a Christmas present, which was a $100 gift certificate to Game Stop. I had fun with Anthony. We would chase each other up and down the escalators at the Pennsylvania Hotel where Curtis and I did our show. This interaction ended as Curtis went back to WABC and I think, in retrospect, my father's subsequent illness and death in April 2014, occupied most of my attention during this period.

I did see Mary again a few months later when I was placed at her firm's table at a dinner hosted by the board of Rabbis honoring Mariano Rivera. At one point, they were auctioning off some box seat tickets to a Yankees game and they got up to about $7,000. I resisted the temptation to jump up, wave my hand, and yell $60,000 just like the last time, being the fine I got for attending the Yankees game without buying the tickets. Before the end of the event, I asked Mary if I could bring some clients into the bank to see if they would be interested in a potential business relationship.

About a month later I was accommodated by Mary and the rest of her team that included Ed Moldaver and Jimmy Lee at Barclays Wealth Management. The meeting went well, and the two potential clients also apprised the bankers that they might be interested in opening up wealth accounts at their firm. At some point, they must have had a lunch and on August 8, 2014, Mary called Tracy Peay, my assistant, to request an immediate meeting. "I could meet him as early as today," she exclaimed. These drop-everything-you're-doing requests come quite often and, to Tracy, I refer to them as drive-bys. I explained to Tracy that I don't do drive-bys and when informing me that she received this call she said; "Governor, we had a drive-by and, now I know what to do, I told her she can call next week and make an appointment." Oh wow! This is the time I really would break my schedule because I adored Mary, so I said to Tracy, "Well, you know, I'm not too busy toward the end of the day, what was the woman's name, Mary Silver? Tell her I'll meet her at 5 o'clock. She can choose the place."

Well, the place turned out to be a well-known restaurant, The Parlor on 90th Street and Third Avenue. Sitting and talking with Mary with the warm sunshine of the late afternoon surrounding the window, I forgot the urgency of the request. We realized we had both worked in radio and traded stories and memories about people we both knew. About half hour into the conversation, Mary moved her glass to the side and said "Governor, this is the reason I needed to see you. Do you know that one of your clients was kicked out of the securities industry for life and the other went to jail for fraudulent stock trading?" This invasion of reality into this comforting exchange of new friendship eclipsed the sunlight and unraveled the strings of my heart. I couldn't believe this. I had taken these people to about ten different venues where all of the proprietors were closer to me than Mary, and yet, this woman, whom I've only seen three times before in my life was the one who alerted me to this problem. They'd never disclosed to me that they had any of these issues. Mary emphasized that they were using my good name for their own gain and eventually my detriment.

After the shock that befell me for about twenty minutes, I then spent the rest of the conversation with Mary trying to determine her availability. Was there a boyfriend? Was there a chance she'll go back to her ex-husband? Just to kind of understand whether or not I might see her again.

On a scale of 1–10, 10 being most available, I assessed Mary at a negative 2. Relationships were far from her mind after an endless and arduous series of events stemming from her divorce battles. I concluded at the end of this session that I had made a wonderful friend. A friend I thought I would keep for the rest of my life because of her sincerity, her character, and her fierce loyalty to someone whom she thought was being exploited. She did say that her partners really liked me and wondered if I had any interest in coming to work for the bank. To this point, I had worked in the law, in education, for a civil-rights not-for-profit, the NAACP, law enforcement, politics, government, and had consulted in real estate, disability rights, and environmental issues. Although decisions regarding finance probably would be my legacy as governor, I had, however, never occupied any position related to finance in any way.

I was now talking to Mary regularly and enjoying the conversations. In one conversation, I found her in Lavallette, New Jersey where she had rented a charming house by the beach for the summer. She told me that the sunset was particularly beautiful that evening and she wished that I could see it. I wondered if she literally wished that I could see it or if she wished I could see it with her. I was hoping for the latter.

On August 24, I boarded a flight to Tel Aviv as part of a goodwill mission led by my longtime friend Joseph Potasnik and the boards of rabbis of New York and New Jersey. I was to meet congressman Peter King at the airport and we would be picked up in Tel Aviv the next morning. I didn't see Peter as I boarded the plane, nor did I see him throughout the flight, even though I walked around the plane once, and I didn't see him when I got off the plane around noon on Monday the 25th. When I got into the airport I found out that the car that was supposed to pick me up has already left and when I called Joseph to tell him I was stuck in the airport, he told me Peter King had taken the car back to the conference. Almost an hour later somebody showed up and brought me to the conference as well, just as Congressman King—also a longtime friend—was speaking at the end of his presentation. "Before we conclude," remarked the moderator, "Governor David Paterson, former governor of New York has joined us, and we wonder if he'd like to say a few words." As I approached the stage, I realized this was a conference about the Department of Homeland Security. Congressman King was head of that committee in the House and had been a guest on my radio show many times after close calls or terrorist incidents. Nevertheless, I chided the audience that I couldn't understand how they could sit there and listen to Congressman King for half an hour and be so complimentary of his credibility when he, as he the most ranking member of Congress in the area of homeland security, couldn't recognize a black blind man on a Jewish airline.

The next day, Tuesday, we were expected to make a trip to Dorot but we were advised that the area was off-limits because of the heavy rocket fire from Hamas during the entire summer of 2014. What we didn't know was that behind the scenes, negotiations were concluding that would bring about a cease-fire in this two-month conflict and, Hamas, knowing they were about to agree to this treaty, was probably emptying the arsenal of rockets before the deadline.

So, we went to see a school in Ashkelon. Although the Israelis were using the "Dome," an incredible technological advancement that wipes 80–90 percent of the rockets out of the sky, it was explained to us that a building had been hit in Ashkelon by a rocket that morning. Some young people said that the rocket hit the building was right next to the building in which they lived. Many of the Rabbis and others in the delegation wanted to go see the building, and although it was not part of our tour and we didn't get the safety briefing or identification of where the nearest shelter was, we boarded the buses and went to the site of the explosion. The mayor of Ashkelon was still there along with reporters and some neighbors looking at the damage. People were taking pictures when, suddenly, the siren went off and we knew that another rocket had been fired.

Our tour guide was mobbed by some of the members of our party who'd rather argue with him about why he didn't know where the shelter was than actually look for one. Scared to my loins, I noticed two young people riding on bicycles who rode right through our group. I surmised that they lived in the area, had heard the sirens, and were heading to a shelter so I started to follow them. "Where are you going, David?" demanded some of my colleagues, who quickly realized that a solution had been discovered and we all got to the shelter. I recall laying on the ground hearing an explosion that must have hit one to one and a half miles away from us and thinking about dinner the night before when a couple of people asked me what it was like to live in Harlem. "Well, I sure wish I was in Harlem right now."

At dinner that evening, someone raised a glass and toasted, "To Governor Paterson, we help him get his bags, we help him to his room, and we help him get his door open, but when a rocket explodes he was going to leave us all there in the dust?" Then, Congressman Peter King congratulated himself for saving my life even though I had insulted him at the event two days before. Talk about the blind leading the blind.

Sitting in my room around midnight, trying to absorb the shock of the explosion and our proximity to it, I thought of Mary, so I called her. I left a message saying, "there were some reports that Congressman Peter King and I were near an explosion in Israel, although the reports don't detail our current whereabouts, I just wanted you to know that I'm safe." I paused. "I don't know why I made this phone call, but I hope you're doing well." I knew why I made the phone call; because that kind of shock erases a gap between one's sense of diplomacy and appropriateness as opposed to their true feelings and, in this case, I had no qualms about revealing them.

On September 9, 2014, exactly two weeks from the date of the explosion, I was at Sam's restaurant meeting with the Barclays team that included Ed Moldaver, Mary Sliwa, and former New York Jets wide receiver Wayne Chrebet. We had come from a police athletic league luncheon and the topic of conversation was whether or not I'd have an interest in coming to their firm. We were trying to figure out a way to accomplish this without taking some of the very difficult securities exams which were required, even for people who had very extensive financial backgrounds. Normally, I would never interrupt a lunch with a phone call, but this time there was an ominous feeling and I answered the phone only to be informed that my best friend, Michael Gaye, had drowned in a swimming accident on the Island of Santorini in Greece while on vacation. Shocking as it was, it surprised me that the information was given to me by Alex Williams, who was a former intern of mine, and I wondered how he would know this. It turned out that Mike had arranged a meeting for Alex and his old girlfriend, about a possible job for Alex over that summer. When she couldn't find my phone number she called Alex, who relayed this horrible tragedy to me.

You know how there are some things about yourself and you don't know why you act this way? Well, one of mine is that, no matter what news I hear, I always believe I can internalize it and address it after I finish whatever task I'm completing at that particular time. This may have been my desire on this occasion, but it clearly wasn't working and the other occupants at the table were noticing more and more.

About ten minutes later, Mary, sitting across from me, got up from her seat walked around to me and put her hand on top of my right hand and said to me, "David, this is not the time to continue this conversation. There's been a tragedy in your life, and we want to help you address it. Ed,"—meaning Ed Moldaver, her partner—"has asked his driver to come to the restaurant. He's outside, ready to take you home or wherever you'd like to go." I got up and excused myself, fighting the urge to completely break down in front of all of them. That evening, a group of us got together to try to comprehend the death of our dear friend Mike, but in the back of my mind was the gentle and supportive way that Mary orchestrated my exit from that lunch.

As a matter of fact, Mary and Ed came to Mike's wake out of respect for me even though they didn't know him, which deeply moved me. When Mary came to the wake, she kneeled at Mike's coffin and said a prayer. She later wondered to me what all the black people thought about this white woman coming and kneeling before Mike and praying, and who this woman might be. I told her, "they probably thought you were one of Mike's girlfriends." Marisol Rodrigues, who is as close to me as Mike was, seemed befuddled by Mary's presence on such a solemn occasion. She always acted as my protector.

A month later, Mary and I were in Ricardo's Steak House on 112th Street and 2nd Avenue in East Harlem. They were having a big celebration for someone's birthday and we got so carried away that we hugged and I kissed her. Nothing was said about the kiss by either of us for about ten days, until we were back at the same restaurant and I came out of the men's room and there was a song on that Mary liked. She grabbed my hand and said, "Hey, let's dance." A friend of mine, looking out for our safety from publicity, broke up the dance and summoned us to go and sit back at our table, which was like being sent to the time-out corner. We then decided we had to discuss where our friendship was going, which is when I came up with about the dumbest thing I'd ever conceived. I suggested that we should go on a date and have a nice time and there was a song I wanted to dance to with her. The song was "Je sais pas" by Celine Dion. This was a date where we could say all these nice things to each other and we could hug and kiss and dance and then we would be, as Mary put it, BFF's, because I was now applying to the Bank and it wouldn't be a great circumstance for the two of us to be seeing each other while at the same job.

BFF time lasted for about ten days when Mary had to go and testify at one of the child support hearings. There wasn't anyone to go with her, and she was quite anxious about the testimony, the media, and the unneeded publicity. I said to her, "Mary I would go with you, but if I go to the courtroom, you'll get more publicity than you've gotten in your life. In fact, you'll go coast to coast. But I will say this. I'll wait for you at Ricardo's,"—the scene of our first kiss—"and when you leave the courtroom, you ride up to the restaurant on the subway and you can sit and vent and talk about anything you want to talk about and I'll be there to listen to you."

As I was listening to myself say this, I knew that was what I call boyfriend talk. So, I had to have a talk with myself to see if I was ready to be somebody's boyfriend again. We went through an almost boyfriend/girlfriend period, until December 19, 2014, when the man who would become my partner at the bank, Ed Moldaver, invited us all to a Christmas party and for some reason there were only two single people there, Mary and myself. So when there was dancing, we danced together, when there was eating we ate together, and he sent us home in a chauffeur-driven van together.

Of course, we didn't tell anyone we were together because we weren't sure how long this was going to last, if this was a good idea, or what we would do if I should be accepted by the bank.

Now look, if there's ever a place you want to go and not lose a secret, please avoid any Black History Month events. I think all of us believe our ethnic group gossips more than all the rest, but I'm convinced that it is black people who gossip the most. When Mary and I came to a black history event, where we were greeted so warmly—I'll never forget it—by the late judge Sheila Abdus-Salaam, a member of New York's court of appeals who died tragically two years later, the story was about to get loose. Sure enough, about six days after the event, I got a call from the *Daily News* stating that "several sources are reporting you are Mary Sliwa's boyfriend." They always try to scare you like there are a hundred people. It's probably one person and I was sure I knew who it was. But I had a problem. We hadn't disclosed to the bank that we were dating and so, if I say yes, it's not very fair to the bank, even though we meant no harm, and if I say, "no I'm not seeing that woman," well let's just say that this approach didn't work out so well for a certain president. So, I came up with what I thought was the greatest quote of my career. I said, "not at this time, but I wouldn't rule it out, because I think she's wonderful."

All the statements were true, and Mary went to Ed Moldaver and told him we were dating, and Ed said, "Please tell the governor, if he asks for your hand, I approve." And so it was that Stifel Nicholas, a St. Louis–based bank, acquired Barclays in December of 2015, and around that time, Mary Sliwa, acquired me in a non-hostile, and quite lovely, takeover. I'd been taken over by her generosity, her warmth, caring about others, and also her open-mindedness about issues that I had brought into her life from my own experiences that she had been largely unaware of to this point.

There was no way to avoid taking the series 7 and series 63 exams to get my license as a registered representative, but Mary was with me every step of the way. The first time I took the series 7, I missed passing it by one question out of 250, literally pegged by 4/10th of one point. Don't they round up when you take these exams? Mary, who was sent by Stifel to observe the exam to make sure everything was right, stopped the exam at one point because the very kind woman who was reading the exam to me was Danish or Norwegian or some indigenous land that produced an accent that made it impossible for me to understand the questions. At some point, she actually gave me the exam itself to read, which if I could, it would have negated the necessity of her being there. This was a real low point for me. I knew that I had studied enough to pass that exam and it was very hard going back to it, even though the next scheduled exam was only three and a half weeks away. But somehow, I pulled myself together and got ready for this second battle with the exam.

Once in an NBA championship series between the Miami Heat and the Dallas Mavericks, Pat Reilly, with his team up three games to two, appeared at the airport for his flight to Dallas with no luggage. The Miami Heat players he was coaching at the time said, "Coach, this is game six. If we lose we're going to have to stay in Dallas for game seven and you have no luggage." Reilly smiled as he quietly offered that he wouldn't be in Dallas more than one day, meaning of course, that he'd planned on having them win game six, as they did, and became the world champions of basketball. My partners, Ed Moldaver and Jimmy Lee had bought me a suit and we agreed that I would wear the suit when I got my license. I chose to wear the suit to the exam, where Mary immediately asked, "Why would you wear the suit before you got the license?" I explained; "I got my license the last time I was here, I'm just back to prove it." I dusted the series seven the second time.

For a few years, I worked with my darling Mary in a "publicly approved" office relationship at Stifel investment bank that yielded professional (and romantic) success, and if you told me this would be happening five years ago, I would have thought I was still suffering from PTGS (Post Traumatic Governor Syndrome). These days, and for as many as I can have, I'm a lucky man because I since made Mary my wife. We were married in 2019 in an eclectically fitting ceremony on a ship on the East River in New York City. The ceremony was officiated by former Mayor of New York, David Dinkins and Rabbi Joe Potasnik; because you can't have too many government officials or religious denominations officiating a wedding such as this. Consequently, in this God-ordained package, came Anthony. I now get to enjoy this young man's company far more regularly and it's like having another son to enrich my life. All in all, I win again.

14

My Vision

Postscript. June 13, 323 BC. I guess by now you have noticed my penchant for dates and times. I am fascinated by the word "when." Measurements such as the circumference of a circle divided by its diameter, known as pi, interest me as well. I can recite the value of pi into over one thousand digits upon request. I think this is just my attempt to bring order to life's otherwise chaotic and mysterious experiences.

Most people revere Einstein's theory of relativity, even though they haven't the foggiest idea of how to explain it. Einstein himself, in spite of four revolutionary and mind-bending theories that he published to the chagrin of his colleagues, always believed that every physical activity had order at its heart. This is why he firmly resisted the elements of quantum physics and its father, the physicist Max Planck. Subsequently, research relegated Einstein's notion of predictability to be obsolete, and in the end, there is no end to pi. But just one more time let me pretend that there is, the affirmation date marks the demise of Alexander the Great, the famed ruler of Macedonia. Assuming the crown in 336 BC upon the murder of his father Philip the second, Alexander immediately bolstered the northernmost borders of Macedonia and then went on to unify the city states of Greece, reestablish the Corinthian league, and conquer Persia and Asia Minor. While attempting to annex Rome and Carthage to his empire, he died of malaria in Babylon, which is now Iraq. But what may be more interesting than the study of Alexander's military victories is an examination of his understanding of reality.

After a series of successful invasions in 335 BC, it became clear to Darius III, the king of Persia, that he and his country were likely next on Alexander's list. Galled at the audacity of the young king who had yet to celebrate his twenty-first birthday, Darius sent him a gift for this occasion. It was a little ball, the likes of which children would play with, and the gift was accompanied by a note; "To Alexander. Please enjoy this gift, which is age appropriate for you, and stay out of the adult affairs of the state." Alexander read the note and then proceeded to expand some territories beyond the northern border of Macedonia. You see, you get up in the morning and check your emails. Alexander got up in the morning and took over places.

Eventually, he got around to sending a note back to Darius, which was one of appreciation. "Thank you for this ball which I see as a replica of the world that I will inherit," Alexander responded. By 331 BC, Alexander was now the king of Persia and Darius had disappeared.

Here again we shouldn't as much appreciate Alexander's brilliance as a tactician in war or his glib intellect—evidenced by his writing—it's simply that Alexander knew the world was round. So did Darius. So did everybody in the region. Alexander had a good teacher, you may have heard of him, a guy named Aristotle. Now doesn't this fly in the face of Columbus sailing the ocean blue in fourteen hundred and ninety two or even the adventures of Leif Erikson in 985 AD One wonders how such scientific knowledge could have been lost on the world, anywhere between fourteen and eighteen centuries.

Albert Einstein advanced in one of his theories that time is cylindrical, and it's most likely that—based on his rigorous opposition to the Nazis and outspoken support for all types of equality movements—he wrote a letter condemning the treatment of the Scottsboro Boys, who were young black male children used in scientific experiments. Thus, I hope he would agree, that not only time, but thought, is cylindrical.

Manuscript Found in Accra is a book that chronicles a meeting between a Coptic priest and the residents of Jerusalem, who were fearing the invasion of Israel by French and other European soldiers. This audience is believed to have occurred on July 14, 1099 CE, where the Copt took questions from members of the three religious groups that were trying to save Israel. The three groups happened to be Christians, Muslims, and Jews. Now this is a get-together I'm sorry I missed. Can you imagine it? Jews, Muslims, and Christians trying to save Israel from attack. In response to one of the questions, the Copt said that there are people who draw comfort from so-called wisdom: "wisdom is an accumulation of ideas put together by people who wish to define the world rather than respecting the mysteries of life." Later in the book, he asserted that rules and regulations that are designed to define behavior, conduct, beauty, value, and social standing is what has created a desire to control others that would capture Israel the next day, and assure that there would not be the peaceful coexistence that existed then, for another thousand years.

We live today having inherited a history of renaissance from inventors, scientists, artists, writers, thinkers, and leaders. We have also been the recipients of brutality and degradation from dictators, military crusades, and corrupt rulers who manipulated the perception of reality and even the truth for their own personal benefit. There has been a greater understanding in the current century as we have noticed reprisals against people in power, mostly men, who used their governmental, business, or social power to sexually abuse and intimidate subordinates in the workplace or some social setting. Widespread evidence of child sexual abuse has now even reached the religious sector with victims coming forward whose innocence was betrayed and individuals who would never have attempted to do such, just a short time ago, now do not allow their race, religion, national origin, their sex, or their sexual orientation from participating at all levels of politics, business, government, and even the religious community. Mankind has taken small steps and giant leaps, as Neil Armstrong suggested, but civilization appears to still be in its infancy, staggering and stumbling with surprisingly little improvement.

After the attacks on September 11, there was a semblance of collective energy when people of all faiths and origins absorbed the pain of such unimaginable brutality.

Many, such as I, had to publicly acknowledge that we had not properly assessed the threat of terrorism. However, by the time relief was rewarded, the state of Wyoming received four and a half times the resources per-capita as the State of New York, where more than 2,700 people were killed. Why is that? Maybe because the Vice President lived there.

In the continued suffering experienced in our healthcare system, and the devastating effects on our economy where one-quarter of our workforce became unemployed, here again, partisan concerns have overwhelmed sound judgment. Though it is true that healthcare agencies have been all over the place with their predictions and advisories, are we really going to compare the request for physical distancing and civic shutdowns to the actions of dictators in communist China and the Soviet Union? Really?

As of this writing, nineteen military conflicts currently rage on this planet today. The worst may be occurring in the country of Rwanda. In a speech at the Democratic National Convention in July, 1984, Governor Mario M. Cuomo described America as more divided than ever. As he put it, "Region against region, class against class, the haves against the have-less-ers and the have-nots." Oh governor, what would you say if you hadn't left us less than five years ago? Our country, the greatest country in the world, was founded on the basis of individualism where people were encouraged to explore, to expand, to learn, and to experience. In the movie *The Fountainhead*, Gary Cooper echoes the feelings of Ayn Rand when he suggests that, "Everything we have gained has come from the independent work of independent minds. Every horror and destruction has come from attempts to robotize people, denying thought, denying reason, and denying freedom." But in the present case, we aren't being denied our individual freedom by an evil despot, we're losing our culture and our productivity from a bifurcated demagoguery that is affecting us all. Democrat vs. Republican, the right versus the left, the one percent against the rest of society. We have somehow managed to replace religion with cable televi-sion. The news has replaced WWE wrestling, and Thanksgiving is no lon-ger stressful by the attempt to get the turkey on the table, but more from trying to get idiots to sit around the turkey.

The suggestion could be made to learn to love your enemies because you act just like them. Let me give an example; In 1998 President Clinton was accused of acting inappropriately with an intern. The major women's advocacy groups for whatever reason remained radio silent through the entire impeachment proceeding. Many of them labeled the investigation as a conspiracy that arose from right wing politics. Then, eighteen years later, one month before the presidential election, candidate Donald Trump was accused of similar conduct and was even seen on a video alluding to some of his dalliances. Evangelicals throughout the country, who would have condemned this conduct if it were pretty much anyone else, said practically nothing except for one incident when an evangelical leader on Fox remarked that; "Well maybe he's changed."

Harboring guilt for taking inaction on the issues that were supposed to have had such great value; both sides have attacked others for either the same conduct or covering up conduct without evidence to prove it—because of their need to try to regain their status as advocates for their beliefs. Sometimes adversaries have actually reversed their positions just so they could keep fighting each other. Fifty years ago, conservatives believed that adults eighteen years of age and older should be eligible for a draft to protect the country and the freedom that they enjoy. The Liberals wanted a volun-teer army. Well now we have a volunteer army and the progressive view is that there should be a shared sacrifice among all Americans in protecting the country and that all people should be eligible to serve. Well, isn't that what they contradicted and decried a half century ago? On the other hand, conservatives, rather than claiming victory, have now decided that they like the volunteer army and the battle goes on with the opposites attracting so much that they are now each on the other side.

Now that I have ridiculed everyone else, it's time for my own mea culpa. I predicted to friends that Donald Trump would lose the presidency by 1 percent of the vote. He actually did, but, the Electoral College gave him a substantial victory and those are the rules that we play by. Friends of mine scoffed at my prediction, predicting that Hillary Clinton would win the presidency by 5–10 percent of the vote, but I felt I could read Trump's ambitions. He played to the legitimate angers and frustrations of many Americans. The fear that others would come from foreign territories to take their jobs or abuse their tax money. That the children of today's hardworking Americans would never be able to equal their output in salary or quality of life. Many Americans feel overwhelmed by reduction of quality of life, coupled with inexorable taxation, and in a dramatic, hard-hitting style Trump championed this view in dramatic terms such as *drain the swamp.*

Considering my history and background you would expect that I would denounce such conduct, and I do, except that I have this little problem. A former New York state Attorney General once said at a gathering in Jamaica, Queens that Americans have their differences but there's one thing that we could agree on: we all wanted to get on a boat and come to this great country. This type of ignorance that I have experienced all too often is what inspired me to document the barbaric voyage of black people to the United States and the unprecedented torture that they received when they arrived. As a teenager studying at Columbia University, I was so appalled learning of the hypocrisy of the new world fighting the tyranny of the British government and then imposing a slavery that was ten times worse in their founding constitution. So whenever I heard angry voices, I signed on. From Marcus Garvey and Noble Drew Ali to Malcolm X, I couldn't get enough antagonistic rhetoric.

So who am I to debase followers of the president for fomenting their frustrations at perceived indignity? In the end, who can blame them? No one, but who can remind them? We can. We can remind them of the terrible truth that they and their ancestors stood idly by during two hundred and forty four years of bondage, another hundred years of segregation, and

another half century of mistreatment. But that's not all, most of them justi-
fied it as the wishes of God and supported it with phony references to its
sanction in the Bible. They even condemned the religious leaders who
wanted the constitution to extend protections to all people, women,
African-Americans, and anybody else that resides in this country.

As a contributor to this chaos, I would like to suggest that there be some
inner dialogue that might lead to a pathway from this spiraling acrimony
that is enveloping the world more than any disease or armed conflict:
Education. The word itself, arises from the Latin educo or educandi. It
means to lead out. I see my charge these days not as much as in public service but in contributing to the reconciliation of the divine consciousness.

The philosopher Joseph Campbell wrote that Jean Piaget referenced
this point in writing in the 7th century, and that Pope Gregory the first
alluded to it in the 12th century. It is, that in moments of crisis, the human
consciousness rises to this lofty level. Campbell writes about a police officer
who saw a woman about to jump off of a bridge in Hawaii. Rushing, he isn't
able to stop her, but jumps off the bridge himself to try to assist her when
they both hit the water. A similar incident occurred in New York City in
the year 2000 when an officer basically performed the same function and
helped to save the life of a woman who was about to kill herself. A year later,
343 firemen lost their lives running into the burning towers on September
11th. Police officers, EMS workers, transit workers, and private citizens forgot about their own families, about their well-being, about their dreams and
the preservation of their own life, to try to help others. Piaget actually writes
that, "Crisis ignites that relationship that's deep within our psyche."

On January 1, 2007, a gentleman fell on the tracks in the New York City
subway system due to an illness. Another man jumped down to try to help
the gentleman up but was unable to lift him. The hero lay down on top of
the man holding his shoulders so his convulsions would not make contact
with the oncoming train. The train miraculously rolled over both of them
without any injury to either. A few weeks later, as lieutenant governor, I
welcomed the gentleman, Wes Autrey, to the floor of the New York State
Senate and we all passed a resolution attesting to his bravery. When I went
up to shake his hand he said to me, "Hi David, how are you doing?" I always
knew him as Wes. I never knew his last name but he worked for a not-for-
profit in Harlem that I funded known as CASH (Community Action to
Save Harlem). I said to him,

"Where did you acquire the courage to dive down there and save a man that you've never even met in your life?"

His response was, "I started taking action too quickly to even think about it. I knew I just had to help this gentleman. Who, by the way, happened to be Jewish."

That's what the surviving rescuers from September 11th said. That's what the policemen in Campbell's book, *The Power of Myth*, said after his attempt to rescue the woman in Hawaii. I believe they've said the same thing because they all saw the same light. Some call it God, some call it a higher consciousness, some call it a conversion of mass and energy. Whatever it is, I maintain that it's better than what we've got.

Think of the great songs that people have admired—"More," the theme from the movie *Mondo Cane*. "You are Everything," the great seventies slow-dance song from The Stylistics. "The Greatest Love of All," originally recorded by George Benson but sung better—in my opinion—by Whitney Houston. And finally, "Unconditional" by Dominican singer Prince Royce. As wonderful as these songs are, they suggest to us that we can seek divine inspiration from another human being, which is categorically impossible. Imbuing supernatural powers or effects from being in love with a human being is inappropriate because such a dynamic could only be fulfilled when interacting with the spirit. "You are everything and everything is you" could only be a reference to God. "The Greatest Love of All" is a reference to God, even though Muhammad Ali jokingly pretended it was to him. No doubt Donald Trump believes the song was written for him. Finally, "More than the greatest love the world has known" again, is a spiritual reference. Now I have no quarrel with the authors of such beautiful music that inspires us, but am merely suggesting that the abundant examples in this genre encourage us to an unattainable standard for those with whom we share affection. This same expectation challenges our political leaders, our bosses, our parents, and even ourselves.

The inference that can be drawn is that, even in non-critical moments, many individuals are seeking a reunion with that oneness with other people and spirituality. Though such an ascension is usually ignited by an emergency or a crisis, it's clear that all of us want to be drum majors. The Reverend Dr. Martin Luther King Jr. delivered the "Drum Major Instinct" Sermon on January 15, 1968, just three months before his assassination. In it, he paraphrased the legendary psychologist Alfred Adler, who wrote that all of us wish to be number one. Babies, who are known to be little bundles of joy, are actually little bundles of ego. They are completely self-absorbed. Dr. King added to this: "The drum major instinct is why so many people are 'joiners.' You know, there are some people who just join everything. And it's really a quest for attention and recognition and importance." For example, I wish I had won that election for class president but my opponent, Aleesha, is the best person for the job and I can't wait to work with her. Meanwhile the loser is frustrated that his class colleagues didn't support him. King himself, who won the Nobel Peace Prize in 1964, wondered why he didn't win the prize in 1963. But he persuaded us that there is nothing wrong with wanting to be first in the class, first in business, or first in the heart of another. Citing a biblical reference, his reprieve to all of us is that if you want to be a drum major, your primary mission should be service to others.

Service to others innately involves the understanding of the conditions that may make them feel the ways they do. The acrimony in our national dialogue arises from the fact that everybody thinks they're right, but very few seem to give the respect that we should to embrace our neighbors, with whom we hold disagreement. Otherwise, horrific calamities, like earthquakes and hurricanes, are the only catalysts for serenity and peace. It's always interesting to watch these ecumenical religious conferences where the religious leaders fiercely debate scripture and its meaning, who's right, and who knows God better. While the shamans and the seers of the same religions easily coexist in a united spirit.

I think too much religious discussion has been dedicated to whether or not there is a god and which group of us is his favorite. Albert Einstein believed that the precious balance of the distance of the earth from the sun, the gravity, and the balance of the universe would be so unlikely that the odds would be so prohibitive that there must have had to have been a higher consciousness to organize all of this. Einstein was not big on the God that you prayed to for help on an exam next Thursday. Einstein is credited with this interpretation but in his biography, author Walter Issacson, attributes this to one of Einstein's favorite authors, the Jewish philosopher, Baruch Spinoza who lived from 1632 to 1677. It is written that the famous Hindu leader, Rama Krishna was approached by one of his followers who informed him that she didn't feel God's presence in her life and therefore she didn't feel that she loved God. The rabbi then asked her, "then who do you love?" She responded, "My 6 year old daughter" and he said to her, "Then your service is complete."

Whatever one believes, it is clear to all of us that there is a great mystery beyond our physical appearance in this world, and if the world is what we imagine it to be, then I would feel that we are all destined for a marvelous reunion.

In the movie, *The American President*, Michael Douglas, who plays the president, scolds his staff member, played by Michael J. Fox, on the need for leadership in the country. He compares this excessive need for leadership to people crawling through the desert craving an oasis and when they don't find water, they eat the sand. In October of 2018, explosive devices were placed in the mailboxes of ten prominent Americans, including two ex-presidents. The responses from the president were, as you'd expect, under-whelming and not particularly convincing. One of the targets was a media outlet that couldn't get even a supportive gesture from a rival outlet with a different point of view. But to be fair, two months prior, the *New York Times* printed an article from an unknown White House staff member about how the president was not privy to communications that were intended for his eyes and that staff were plotting behind his back—even to go as far as look-ing at the articles of the 25th Amendment should they feel that he needed to be removed. The president's response is that he was commencing an investigation to find out who those staff members were, and he pledged retribution against them. Many members of the media and different outlets seemed to be cheering these people on as if they were undercover spies hid-ing out in the old Soviet Union. I was not one of them. I was the victim of rogue staff members that took down all references and pictures of me in my own Washington office. One commissioner urged their colleagues not to comply with my requests for lists of employees that might have to be laid off due to budget cuts. When I found out who the staff member was, I fired him, even though I only had seven weeks to go in my term of office. Sorry guys, I'm with Trump on this one.

Let's put aside the discussion about the divine consciousness. We in this country have gotten to a point where we can't even establish a standard that all of us will adhere to in the situations that prevail in our daily lives. Meanwhile, publishers, networks, political consultants, candidates, and the internet profit from the acrimony that has interrupted a national conversa-tion that's needed now more than ever. There are thousands of people working more than one job and still unable to make ends meet, state bud-gets wildly out of balance due to pension debt, more children going without food and shelter than in recent memory, widespread homelessness popping up in our major cities, a raging immigration problem developing from the inability of our leaders to even sit at the table—much less negotiate over it—and a heightened tension on the streets of our cities, rural communities, and all over suburbia as our country struggles to find the peace that we were promised.

A reporter suggested to me that I run for mayor of the city of New York in 2017 and I told him, "I've moved on."

"It's in your blood," he responded.

"I had a transfusion," I said. This was printed on page 6 of the *New York Post* around Memorial Day. Toward the end of 2018, I was approached again by a number of New York's renowned civic leaders to do the same in 2021. I told them I've gotten used to this great feeling I have on Fridays, right before the weekend, as opposed to when I was in office, when Friday was just a day before the two days I worked on the weekends. And I'm not the only one. In spite of the scandals and the disappointing conduct at times, I must say that the best people I ever met in my life came from politics. I have friends in every sector of society, every religious group, every race, every level of wealth, and in the LGBTQ communities. I can't think of a career that would have offered me these opportunities to get to know people in such detail.

Now I will admit, some of the worst people I ever met in my life were also in politics, but there were surprisingly few of them. Council members, village trustees, staff to legislators, researchers, and press secretaries. They work all hours all days of the week. Sometimes, this service infringes upon family life and marriages, and sometimes the marriages haven't worked out. But they work very hard and are substantially underpaid. Every time they try to get a pay raise the public rebels against them, and although the public wouldn't pay for the raise, they've paid for the absence of many good people who've gone on to other careers that are far more lucrative and satisfying. The caliber of legislators in Albany, in my opinion, has diminished by 30 percent from when I started in 1985, and there are far more alternatives for those who were attracted into the profession years ago.

I MARRIED THE love of my life, and Mary and Anthony have made me part of their family, and that's pretty cool. Ashley and Andrew Greenspan—my daughter and son in-law—made me a grandfather, and I couldn't be more thrilled. It's fun watching my son, Alex, grapple with the fact that he's one of the most gifted people that I've ever met, and as for me, I learned that the toughest of times bring out the best in people. The sacrifice that my parents made to have me attend public school in Long Island so that I wouldn't be in a limited environment is the only reason that you're reading my notes right now. My lifelong struggle of having some sight, but not really being sighted enough to negotiate life's twists and turns, has made me a more creative person over the years. My own failure to find remedies in college and law school, causing me to leave both institutions and then extending the pain of that period by not seeking help, has made me keenly aware of the problems that many of my constituents had where they not only were at times unlucky or mistreated, but now lacked the self-esteem to find ways to improve their situations. Discrimination I've felt, either for being black or blind or sometimes not realizing which one was causing it, prepared me for some of the merciless, malicious, and orchestrated attacks that I endured as governor of the state of New York. There were a lot of things I would change if I could do it over again, but I'm pretty happy the way things have worked out. So, I don't think I really need another foray into the battles of government and the electoral process. Suffice it to say, I don't need an encore.

On April 11, 1962 I watched the first game ever played by the New York Mets, a game they lost to the St. Louis Cardinals 11 to 4, and I'm still watching. They better get it together real soon, because I'm getting restless wanting one of my sports teams to win something and win something soon. If not, I'm going to have to find another form of entertainment. And who knows, maybe that entertainment will be public service. I think there are two ways to operate in politics. One is to find what people hate and to take advantage of it, the other is to find out what people love and encourage them to believe in it more than they do.

A radio host named Joe Frank who broadcast on New York's local NPR station, told a story about a rabbinical class in which the professor asked his students to define when daybreak occurs. One of the students raised his hand and said, "Daybreak occurs when you can tell the difference from a distance between the face of a dog and the face of a lamb."

The rabbi congratulated the student for his creativity but told him that wasn't the answer that he was looking for. After a moment of thought a second student raised his hand and said, "Well actually, it is when there is enough daylight that has arisen from the sunrise that you can see the lines on your hand."

The rabbi pondered and was impressed with the thought, but here again explained this was not the answer he was looking for. Finally, a woman student in the rabbinical class offered that "It isn't daylight but that day break occurs from the sweetest sounds of the birds."

The teacher agreed that was a wonderful moment to hear but wasn't the right answer. When all the students had given up they asked the rabbi, "when does Daybreak occur?"

His answer: "Dawn occurs when you look into the faces of all the people around you and see them as your brothers and sisters. Until that time we are all in the dark."

I was taught to love my neighbors like they are ourselves, but my experiences in life revealed that we should love our neighbors because they are ourselves.

The End?